# Jewellery

## OF TIBET AND THE HIMALAYAS

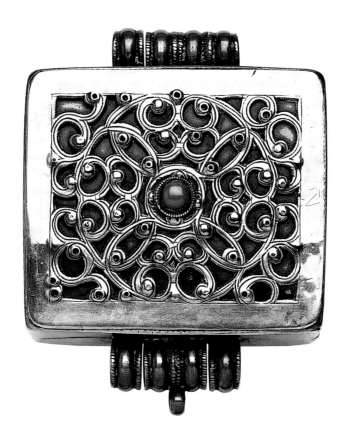

# Jewellery

## OF TIBET AND THE HIMALAYAS

John Clarke

V&A Publications

First published by V&A Publications, 2004
Reprinted 2008

V&A Publications
160 Brompton Road
London SW3 1HW

Designed by Nigel Soper
V&A photography by Ian Thomas of the V&A Photographic Studio

ISBN 978 1 851 77423 4

A catalogue record for this book is available from the British Library

Front jacket illustration: Woman's waist ornament (plate 60)
Back jacket illustrations (clockwise from top left): Details from
plates 109, 69, 62, 44
Frontispiece: Ceremonial amulet box (plate111)

Printed in Hong Kong

V&A Publications
160 Brompton Road
London SW3 1HW
www.vam.ac.uk

# Contents

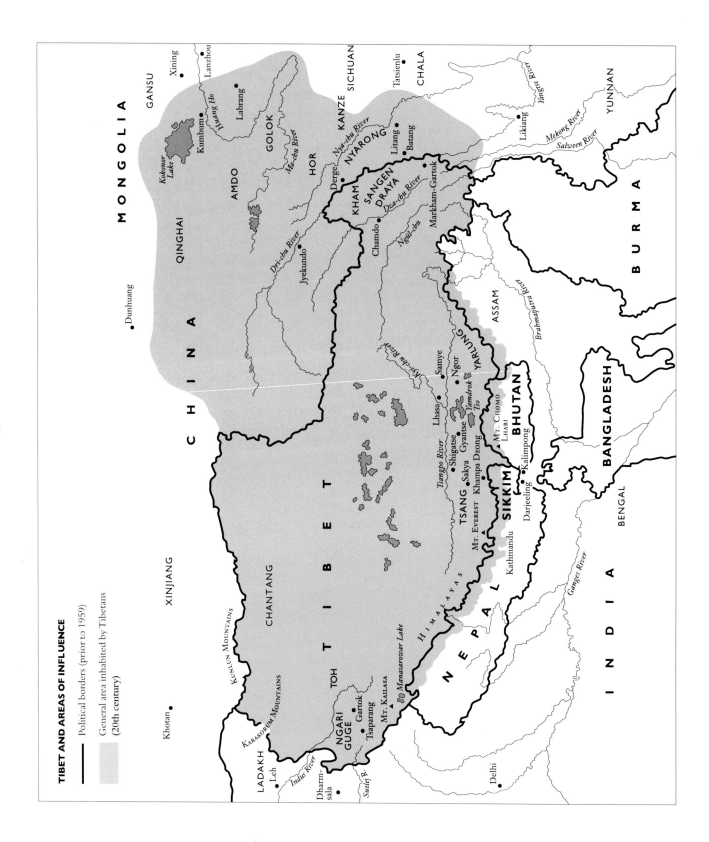

—— Political borders (prior to 1959)

General area inhabited by Tibetans
(20th century)

MONGOLIA

GANSU

Xining

Lanzhou

Labrang

Kumbum

*Huang Ho*

Kokonor
*Lake*

AMDO

GOLOK

*Ma-chu River*

HOR

*Nya-chu River*

KANZE

SICHUAN

Tatsienlu

CHALA

Derge

KHAM

NYARONG

Litang

Batang

SANGEN
DRAYA

*Dza-chu River*

Markham-Gartok

Likiang

YUNNAN

*Yangtse River*

*Mekong River*

*Salween River*

QINGHAI

*Dri-chu River*

Jyekundo

Chamdo

*Ngül-chu*

BURMA

Dunhuang

CHINA

*Kyi-chu River*

Samye

Ngor

*Tsangpo River*

Lhasa

*Brahmaputra River*

ASSAM

YARLUNG

Shigatse

Gyantse

*Yamdrok
Tso*

Sakya

TSANG

Khampa Dzong

Mt. CHOMO
LHARI

BHUTAN

BANGLADESH

Mt. EVEREST

NEPAL

SIKKIM

Kalimpong

Darjeeling

BENGAL

Kathmandu

*Ganges River*

INDIA

KUNLUN MOUNTAINS

XINJIANG

T I B E T

CHANTANG

*HIMALAYAS*

Delhi

Khotan

KARAKORUM MOUNTAINS

TOH

NGARI
GUGE

Gartok

Tsaparang

Mt. KAILASA

*Manasarowar Lake*

LADAKH

Leh

Dharm-
sala

*Indus River*

*Sutlej R.*

# Preface

Despite an ever growing interest in the arts of the Himalayan region it is only in the last two decades that any serious studies of its jewellery have been made. Two pioneering works in German[1] were followed by Jane Casey Singer's *Gold Jewellery of Tibet and Nepal* and perhaps the first comprehensive survey of Nepalese jewellery by Hannelore Gabriel in *Jewellery of Nepal*. A number of museums have also published parts of their collections in recent catalogues.[2] Perhaps inevitably, catalogues of individual institutions or private collections tend to reflect respectively the biases and strengths of their holdings or the approach of a collector, and therefore to give a partial picture. The aim of this work therefore is to give a balanced and accessible survey of the subject, drawing for the first time on all the major British national collections which until now have remained mostly unpublished and unseen. A selection of the most significant and visually pleasing pieces has been made from such collections which include the Victoria and Albert Museum, British Museum, National Museum of Scotland, Liverpool City Museum, Ashmolean Museum, Pitt Rivers Museum and the Cambridge Museum of Archaeology and Anthropology.

The core of several of these collections takes us back to an early period of contact between Britain and the Himalayan countries. In the case of the East India Company Museum, whose jewellery collections now form part of the Asian Department of the V&A, the earliest traceable purchases were made during the 1850s in Kathmandu, Sikkim and the newly acquired trading town of Darjeeling. Another significant group of jewellery and other objects was brought out of Tibet as the result of the expedition of 1904 led by Colonel (later Sir) Francis Younghusband. Objects acquired by officers, soldiers and other diplomatic personnel stationed at the trading posts, established in Tibet as a result of the expedition, gradually entered western collections over the next decades, were sold on at auction and snapped up by museums. The Nepalese jewellery held in western museums tends to consist predominantly of stone-inlaid ceremonial pieces made by Newar goldsmiths. The visual impact of such objects evidently appealed to nineteenth-century museum curators but their preponderance means that no meaningful coverage of the other styles worn in Nepal is possible. It therefore seemed appropriate to concentrate on Newar jewellery in the Nepalese section here rather than to attempt a wider survey.

This book brings together recent research on the history of jewellery in the region, on regional styles and on the production techniques of goldsmiths, with information on the religious imagery found on pieces, the folklore surrounding stones and the part jewellery played in Tibetan and Nepalese society. This provides the reader with an understanding of the contextual background which should enrich the visual appreciation that these pieces naturally evoke. The far-flung trade routes by which coral, amber, pearls and turquoise travelled to Tibet and Nepal from Europe and Iran is a fascinating aspect of the subject that links our own cultures to the heart of Asia. The wearing of traditional jewellery still remains a living tradition in many areas as contemporary photographs testify. It is hoped that the visual record of these photographs, together with groups of the objects themselves, will give a real feel for the distinct regional styles worn throughout this huge area which is virtually the size of western Europe.

## Note on names in the Tibetan language

The phonetic versions of Tibetan names have been given throughout the text. Transliterated equivalents (according to the Wylie system) may be found in the glossary alongside the phonetic versions.

Unless otherwise indicated, all foreign terms in italics are in the Tibetan language. The exceptions are Sanskrit (denoted by S), Newar (denoted by N), and Chinese (denoted by C). In Chapter 6 all terms in italics are Newar.

# The History and Culture of the Himalayas

THE WESTERN STEREOTYPE of Tibet as a cultural island isolated in Asia is in many ways the opposite of historical reality. Already by early in the seventh century, when it enters recorded history, Tibet had become a great trading nation and was exporting the salt, wool, musk, yak tails and horses that are a feature of its later trade, receiving in return Chinese silk, spices and brick tea. From this period onwards Tibetan culture was shaped by its assimilation of cultural, artistic and religious influences from its neighbours, especially India, Nepal and China. Under a succession of powerful king/emperors, or *tsenpo,* Tibet emerges during this period as a unified warlike state with an expansionist military policy dominating large parts of Asia beyond its borders.[1] During these centuries Buddhism, in both its Indian Mahayana and probably Chinese Ch'an forms was introduced, although it met opposition from the indigenous animistic religion, later called Bon, with its belief in spirits of the air, rivers, lakes and earth.[2]

The Mahayana teachings that became predominant were brought mainly from India and Nepal. They stressed the ideal of the Bodhisattva, a being who eschewed Buddhahood in order to keep being reborn in the world in order to guide others towards enlightenment. There were also more advanced and secret Tantric or Vajrayana practices that were considered a fast but dangerous path to enlightenment involving visualization, breath control and the use of mantras or magical sounds. Tibetan translators and practitioners who returned from India gathered their own students and their successors eventually formed the nucleus of three new monastic orders between the eleventh and thirteenth centuries.

From the twelfth century onwards the orders began to become centres of political power in their own right and developed rivalries which helped keep power largely decentralized until the mid-seventeenth century when one order, the Gelukpas, became dominant. In 1578 the leader of the order,

*Woman's waist ornament from Lhasa (plate 60)*

I. JEWELLERY DECORATING THE JOBO IMAGE
JOKHANG TEMPLE, LHASA, 1980s

The earliest known set of ornaments
decorating this most sacred of Tibetan
images, brought from China in the 7th
century, were donated by one of Tibet's
greatest religious leaders Je Tsongkhapa
in 1409. The crown, earrings and
breastplate on the front of the image
today were taken from another statue
to replace the original, lost or destroyed
during the Cultural Revolution. They are
thickly encrusted with women's *ga'us*, *dzi*
beads and multiple settings of corals,
turquoises and pearls.
Photograph © Ian Cumming/Tibet
Images

the abbot of Drepung monastery, Sonam Gyatsho, was given
the honorific title 'Ta Le', the Mongolian equivalent of his
name 'Ocean of Wisdom', by his Mongolian supporter Altan
Khan. So began the tradition of the Dalai Lamas who under
the fifth Dalai Lama in the mid-seventeenth century eventually
unified secular and religious power. The theocratic
government established then survived largely intact until nine
years after the Chinese invasion in 1950.

China exercised a loose but real control over Tibet during
the nineteenth century and the conservative monastic
establishment readily accepted its exclusionist policy which
they saw as protecting religion. The exclusion before 1950 of
all but a very little modern western influence kept Tibet
politically and technologically where it had been for centuries.
Wealth continued to be concentrated in a small number of
immensely rich noble families whose estates provided surplus
agricultural produce that could be sold for profit. In addition
the nobles, together with the monasteries and the two greatest
political figures in Tibet, the Dalai Lama and the Panchen
Lama, engaged in the lucrative trade in Chinese tea and silks.

When the Chinese communists came to power in 1949
and declared their aim the 'liberation' of Tibet, its past
isolationism meant that it had only a small and ill-equipped
army and almost no international support. After a brief
campaign, communist forces entered Lhasa in 1950. At first
they worked with the existing government but by the mid-
1950s were introducing ever more repressive laws. Finally a
spontaneous uprising occurred in Lhasa in 1959 when it
appeared that the Dalai Lama's life was threatened. It was put
down harshly and with great loss of life[3] by the army and from
this point on China imposed direct rule, dissolving the old
government structure. The destruction of monasteries and
traditional lifestyles was well underway by the early 1960s but
was frighteningly intensified during the Cultural Revolution
(1966-77). Since then 120,000 Tibetans have followed the
Dalai Lama into exile, settling in India and throughout the
world and establishing a seat of government in exile at
Dharamsala in Himachal Pradesh. There and elsewhere in
India they have made a determined attempt to re-found
monasteries and to maintain and transmit their traditional
culture to new generations. Inside Tibet the most repressive
policies were repealed in 1980, allowing a measure of religious
freedom and the entrance of monks into the remaining few
monasteries. However, Tibetan culture and religion remain
threatened by the mass migration of Han Chinese and the
suffocatingly tight government control of religion.

## An Introduction to the Regions of Tibet

The present day borders of the Tibetan Autonomous Region, created in 1964 by the Chinese administration, are far narrower than Tibet's traditional borders. To the north and east large parts of the former Tibetan provinces of Amdo and Kham are now amalgamated with the Chinese provinces of Gansu, Qinghai and Sichuan. Historically Tibetan culture spread still further beyond even its pre-Chinese takeover limits. In spite of such recent losses the present TAR still covers over one million square kilometres, an area roughly equivalent to Britain, France and Germany combined, but with a population of about ten million.

Tibet, literally at the heart of Asia, lies sandwiched between two major Asian powers, India to the south-west and China to the east. Names such as 'roof of the world' are justified by Tibet's sheer height, with most of the country lying at over 3,500 metres.[4] Tibet is ringed on three sides by some of the highest mountains in the world (see map). It contains a number of distinctly different and varied landscapes created by differences in land height and rainfall. Across the length of northern Tibet from the western almost to the eastern border stretches a vast wilderness area of high-altitude plateau, the Changtang, lying mostly above 5,000 metres and thickly set with salt-bearing lakes. Too high and cold for agriculture, its vast grasslands and deserts are inhabited here and there by nomads who rely on their herds for survival. The former province of Kham is an area of wide, fertile pastures and river valleys watered by the monsoons of nearby Assam and Yunnan. Four of Asia's major rivers, the Salween, Mekong, Yangtse and Yalung flowing south-east into China proper, create river valleys that get progressively narrower and deeper towards the east and eventually turn into gorges. Throughout the region agricultural land alternates with expanses of high grassland,[5] the home to nomads with their herds of yak, goats and sheep. Black nomad tents made of woven yak hair dot the grasslands while in the valleys substantial stone or earth and wood houses provide the dwellings for farmers.

The men of Kham have long had the reputation as the best warriors in Tibet, although they are also often characterized by other Tibetans as quarrelsome. A sword was typically carried by men, not only in times of war but in peace to protect themselves from the robbers who were especially endemic in the nomadic grasslands to the north and east (plate 77). Despite the often turbulent nature of the border, Kham in particular was a prosperous area, famous for its metalwork and the home of a number of important monasteries such as Derge and Chamdo.

In the north-east the Changtang merges with large areas of rolling grasslands inhabited by nomadic populations in present-day Qinghai province (former Amdo). Finally there is the economic and cultural heartland of Tibet, lying along the fertile valley of the Yarlung Tsangpo to the south. Within this valley, with its strong trade links to India and Nepal in the south, lie many of Tibet's most important monasteries and towns, including the capital itself, Lhasa.

## The Himalayan Kingdoms: Ladakh, Sikkim, Bhutan and the Western Himalayas

The Himalayas contain some of the highest mountains in the world, which in some parts of Bhutan rise abruptly from the Indian plains from only 150 metres above sea level to several peaks above 7,000 metres. Within the wide range of physical environments it is possible to discern three broad climatic areas defined by altitude within long sections of the Himalayan chain. The lowest of these three step-like zones supports lush tropical forest which extends to about 1,500 metres. For the most part such lowland areas have not been settled by Tibetan peoples who historically had little resistance to malaria and other tropical diseases. From about 1,500 to 3,000 metres there stretches a temperate zone covered by the dense forest still retained in many areas of Sikkim and over half of Bhutan. Here maize and wheat can be grown and, up to a limit of 2,000 metres, wet rice planted in terraced fields in the valley bottoms.[6] Herders maximize grazing by taking their flocks and herds to high pastures in the early summer and down to low ones in the autumn. Higher up, from 3,000 to 5,000 metres, is an Alpine zone in which climate and altitude are almost identical to those of the Tibetan plateau itself. Lahaul, Spiti, much of Kinnaur and the northern border regions of Sikkim, Bhutan, Nepal and Arunachal Pradesh all share these harsh high-altitude desert conditions. The quintessentially Tibetan yak, *Bos grunniens*, can only survive well at above 2,500 metres and is most at home in the high zone. Single-handedly this animal provides many of life's necessities: butter, milk and meat, wool for making ropes, blankets and tents, leather for the soles of boots and, equally importantly, transportation and a means of ploughing.

Tibetan populations with their distinctive Buddhist religion and culture extend well beyond the twenty-first-century borders of Tibet into the high alpine valleys along the 2,400-kilometre length of the Himalayan chain. Known to the Nepalese and Indians as Bhotia, 'Bhot' meaning Tibet, these groups speak dialects of Tibetan, use Tibetan script and share the Tibetan physical characteristics. The spread of such Tibetan Buddhist populations is the result of over a thousand years of sporadic migrations of small groups fleeing persecution or in search of new living space. In Ladakh these movements may have started during the middle of the eight century when Tibet established control of the territory[7]. Towards the middle of the ninth century western Bhutan was being settled by Tibetans who, according to one Tibetan source, were imperial border troops who decided to settle rather than return to Tibet at the time of the collapse of the Tibetan monarchy in 842.[8] The ancestors of the Namgyal dynasty of Sikkim originally came from eastern Tibet in the thirteenth century[9] while in 1533 other groups from Kham colonized parts of the northern Nepalese regions becoming known as Sherpas, their name *sharpa* meaning easterner.[10] Migrations continued throughout the Himalayas until at least the seventeenth century, although in many cases we do not know when they occurred.

Cross-border trade through the river valleys that flow down to the Indian plains, as well as trade and religious contacts across the Nepalese border, have helped to maintain the links between the Tibetan homeland and such outlying communities sharing the same basic language and religion. Although Tibet has come to be the dominant influence on the cultural and religious life of the region, the existence of many indigenous peoples and of immigrants from central Asia, India and Nepal, who to varying degrees have intermixed with Tibetan populations, has created a vibrant and richly complex picture. Tibetans commonly refer to such groups as 'Monpa', non-Buddhist lands south of the Himalayas being historically referred to as 'Mon'.[11] Some of these, such as the original inhabitants of Sikkim and western Bhutan the forest-dwelling Lepchas and Limbus, maintained elements of their own languages, dress and animistic religion.

There were also ancient immigrants such as the Dards who by the first century CE may have already arrived from central Asia to settle in the upper Indus Valley of Ladakh.[12] Much more recently, since the late nineteenth century, large numbers of Hindu Nepalese immigrants have settled in Sikkim, first encouraged by the British who had established a protectorate over the country in 1890. There are also many Indian Himalayan areas, such as Kinnaur, where Indian populations have intermarried with Tibetans giving rise to varying degrees of cultural blending. Altitude and proximity to the Tibetan border are usually the factors determining ethnic make-up and religion: the nearer one approaches the plateau the more likely is it that one will find Tibetan Buddhism and culture.[13] In the south-west, the network of mountains and narrow valleys which form Lahaul and Spiti (Himachal Pradesh) are another such area. Today, although Hinduism is also found there, Tibetan culture and religion predominates in Lahaul, centering on the Chandra and Bhaga Valleys, and in Spiti a subsidiary valley to the Sutlej. In Kinnaur, in the 100-kilometre-long section of the upper Sutlej Valley, Buddhism also predominates in the populations living in the northern third running up to the Tibetan border.

Along the Himalayan chain lie the present-day Buddhist kingdom of Bhutan and the two former kingdoms of Sikkim and Ladakh. Ladakh encloses the most westerly corner of the high Tibetan plateau and the upper reaches of the Indus River. Its 155,000 square kilometres of high-altitude desert has one of the lowest population densities in the world with around one person per square kilometre.[14] Most settlement lies along two parallel valleys, that of the Indus and of the Zanskar to the south. In these areas oasis-like farming settlements vividly dot with bright green the dry grey-brown surrounding landscape, the fertile alluvial soil being brought to life by the ingenious use of irrigation channels fed by water from glaciers and streams at a higher level. The often substantial mud-brick houses stand in small fields enclosed by stone walls shaded here and there by willows and poplars. To the east lies the start of the high desert plateau, the Changtang, a bare and windswept landscape where water freezes at night even in midsummer. This area forms part of western Tibet and like it is inhabited by nomads raising sheep and goats to produce wool.

Ladakh's continuous trade and religious links with western and central Tibet[15] have fostered its Tibetan culture while politically, from the mid-tenth century until 1834, it has remained a separate Buddhist kingdom. However, for much of its history Ladakh has remained at the crossroads of several cultures with India to the south, Muslim Kashmir and Pakistan to the north-west and Tibet to the east. It has suffered repeated attacks by more powerful Muslim states surrounding it and has come under their political control for long periods but, beneath a nominal adherence to Islam forced upon it, has mostly remained Buddhist.

Ladakh lay at the centre of trade routes connecting the Punjab in northern India with Yarkand and Khotan in central Asia, feeders to the earlier central Asian silk route. Ladakh was mostly an entrepôt centre for the trade between India and central Asia and Tibet. Through these routes went Indian products such as tea, textiles, spices and coral to central Asia

A view showing the gilded
roofs of the most important
temples in Tashilunpho
monastery. Below it is part
of the city of Shigatse and
beyond that the Yarlung-
Tsangpo Valley.

and Tibet while in the other direction came Chinese and
central Asian silks, silver, carpets and Tibetan wool and gold.[16]
At Indian Independence in 1947, the Maharaja of Kashmir,
who controlled Ladakh, seceded it to India but only a year later
Pakistan, who claimed the territory, invaded Baltistan in
northern Ladakh. Although this territory was lost, the
heartlands of Ladakh were saved. The area has remained
disputed to the present day, both by Pakistan and China who
in 1962 invaded and took control of part of the high plateau
in the east.[17]

Adjoining Nepal's eastern edge is the former kingdom of
Sikkim. Independent from 1642 until 1975, it is now absorbed
into India. Its people are a mixture of indigenous groups such as
the Lepchas, Tibetans and recently arrived Nepalese immigrants.
To the east Sikkim is divided from Bhutan by a wedge of Tibetan
territory, the Chumbi Valley,[18] which forms a natural corridor
that rises to the plateau between the two countries. This became
one of the principal trade routes with Tibet after the British
established a trade station at Yatung in 1903/4.

The kingdom of Bhutan bounded in the north by Tibet
and in the south by the Indian states of Assam and West Bengal
is almost exactly the size of Switzerland, 46,500 square
kilometres, but with a population of just under 600,000. Most
settlement is concentrated in its middle temperate zone at
1,500–3,000 metres, a landscape of green valleys surrounded
by hills and mountains. Much of the country's ancient primary
forest cover remains while in valleys below rice, barley and
wheat grow in small fields. The distinctive, chalet-style,
Bhutanese houses with their overhanging roofs of wood
shingles, or more recently of shiny corrugated iron, are
scattered amongst rice paddies.

Bhutan became a separate entity politically as the result of
a dispute in 1616 between rivals for the leadership of the
Drukpa Kagyupa which forced the Lama Nawang Namgyal
to flee Tibet and establish his own government. Since the
1950s Bhutan has followed the path of a separate and gradual
development to safeguard its unique Buddhist heritage and
prevent the type of westernization that mass tourism brings.
This has meant that the country remains closed to mass
tourism but it has sought western expertise on education,
health and communications in order to create the foundations
of a modern state.

2

# Why was Jewellery worn?

BEYOND THE APPEAL OF THEIR LUSTROUS SURFACES and glowing colours, pieces of Himalayan jewellery have the power to reveal intimate facets of the lives of those who owned and wore them. Like a tiny mirror reflecting a society often distant in time and space, a single piece can reveal its wearer's sex, their regional origins, position in society and way of life as well as allowing us glimpses of religious preoccupations and beliefs.

Most jewellery made from precious metals was considered auspicious and luck bringing in Tibet and many pieces were also believed to have strong amuletic properties. In southern Tibet it was considered bad luck for a woman to go without her hair ornaments except at times of mourning.[1] Up until the 1950s this led to women sleeping in their enormous headdresses (plate 64) a practice which necessitated lying with them outside of the bed.[2] There were certain ceremonies that were thought to be more effective when women wearing jewellery were present while to give a woman a precious stone on her betrothal was believed to protect her during pregnancy. There were also a few items that were worn specifically to guard against spiritual evil such as the large ivory rings worn, on the thumb of the left hand, by men in the past to protect them against witches[3]. Tibetan belief also held that without pierced ears one risked being reborn as an animal such as a donkey in a future life. This led men, who normally wore one earring in the left ear, to also wear a small stud of polished turquoise in the right. An equally universal practice which continues today is the use of amulets contained in decorative boxes or *ga'us*. *Ga'us* were used in all areas influenced by Tibetan culture and by almost everyone both rich and poor and are still worn by many Tibetans today. The word *ga'u* means simply case or container for relics and must be distinguished from the amulet, or *ten,* within. Both Buddhists and the

Official's hair amulet box (plate 48)

3. MAN WEARING A BOX *ga'u* AT A FESTIVAL
Derge, 2003

Although often slung across the left
shoulder at the front of the body, amulet
boxes are sometimes worn in this way at
the side. The type of silk sash seen here is
also sometimes used instead of leather
straps. In the past it was common to
possess several *ga'us* and quite usual for a
man to carry five or six on a journey.[1]
But in the early 20th century Tibetan
travellers were sometimes seen carrying
as many as twelve facing at the front, back
and sides, to protect themselves from evil
that might come from any direction.
They might even be attached to the
leading animals in pack trains to protect
the whole caravan.[2]

followers of the indigenous Bon religion[4] wear *ga'us* to protect
them against the attacks of capricious nature spirits such as the
*lu* living in the waters of lakes and rivers, mountain spirits and
the *sa dag* or 'Lords of the Soil'. Although peaceful it is believed
that such entities can become angered by disturbances or
pollution of the earth or waters (page 40). In addition to
Buddhist deities and rolls of printed prayers, any objects that
have been worn by or come into contact with revered
religious figures, such as scraps of clothing or bits of silk
presentation scarves known as *katag*, are highly regarded for
their protective power. However, no amulet is regarded as
effective unless activated by a lama through prayers and
offerings to the Gods and through the faith of its wearer.

The powerful protective and medicinal qualities of stones
(chapter 3) served to increase the spiritual benefits given by
jewellery such as *ga'us*. The rosary, or *treng wa,* was also charged
with spiritual power by its constant religious use. While fleeing
on horseback from the invading Chinese, Jamyang Sakya
dropped her finest jewelled rosary. Unable to dismount because
hotly pursued, she quickly reasoned that 'the prayer beads
protective function would prevent our enemies from pursuing
us beyond the point where they had been dropped'.[5]

Jewellery and clothing in Tibet formed the two most
obvious and visible indicators of wealth and social position. In
many instances, particularly if you were a government official,
rank determined what you were allowed to wear. But there
remained plenty of scope for those with money but without
official rank to show off. This led to wide differences in
richness of ornamentation and finish within the same basic
type of ornament according to the economic status of its
owner. Thus the wealthiest women from southern Tibet, or
*Tsang*, who might be the wives of rich merchants and not
necessarily the nobility, swathed their hooped headdresses in
strings of pearls (plate 64) in addition to studding them with
corals and turquoises. At the other end of the social spectrum,
the poorest woman wore a similar wooden hoop, set with
perhaps just a few small turquoises or corals, or simply a felt
circle set with stones worn around the head. Other ornaments
too such as the *ga'u* or amulet box were also commissioned
according to the financial resources of the patron.

For men similarly jewellery and ornament were statements
of their position in society. Together with his gun, sword and
saddle, a man's amulet box or *ga'u* was a status symbol on
which he lavished as much wealth as possible. If he was an
official in the Lhasa government, he was required to wear the
indicators of his rank which were highly regulated according

4. OFFICIAL'S HAT
SILK BROCADE, COPPER-GILT,
TURQUOISE.
Lhasa, c. 1930s
16 cm high, 33 cm diam.

One visible and very specific
symbol of rank was the gold hat
finial called *trudok* or *shalok* which
decorates this brocade-covered hat
with its fringe of silk tassels. These
were detachable and could be worn
on both winter and summer hats[3]
by officials of the fourth rank
upwards. The approximately 70 to
80 fourth-rank officials who were
responsible for many of the routine
duties of government wore
turquoises such as this.[4]
National Museums Liverpool

to position. What was worn depended on which of the eight levels of government officialdom he belonged to. One of the most visible insignia of office for all lay officials was the thin pencil-shaped earring, or *sochi*,[6] (plate 49) and the stone-set, gold hat finial (plate 4) called *trudok* or *shalok*.[7] The particular stone worn on the top of a hat or hat finial showed the wearer's rank. The Prime Minister, a first-rank official, wore a pearl at the top of his finial, the four cabinet ministers, of second rank, wore rubies while lay officials of the third rank, who were the heads of government departments, wore coral hat ornaments. When hats were not worn, lay officials wore a small, oval, turquoise-studded amulet box in the queue of their braided hair called *tagab*[8] (plates 47, 48).

An official's wife too had to be provided with jewellery appropriate to her husband's rank. There were a few ornaments that were considered essential for self-respecting women of any but the poorest class in Lhasa. These consisted of the horned coral-and-pearl-covered headdress or *patruk* (plates 53, 55), the long lotus-bud-shaped earrings or *akor* (plate 56), the *ga'u* or amulet box and the *trakey* or string of pearls.[9] Women would not often be seen without at least earrings and an amulet box. The next most eye-catching element of female ornament was the square or pillow-shaped, jewel-set amulet boxes or *ga'us* (plates 51, 52, 54) strung on necklaces of corals, turquoises and pearls. Even down to the 1950s, men and women of the ruling class were obliged to wear full sets of appropriate ornaments for important occasions and a woman could be fined for not wearing her headdress during the New Year ceremonies.[10]

There was much jewellery that was worn by both sexes and several common types of amulets, rings and earrings were seen adorning both men and women. In general men's rings and amulet cases tended to be larger and heavier versions of women's but were, as in the case of the saddle ring, often of the

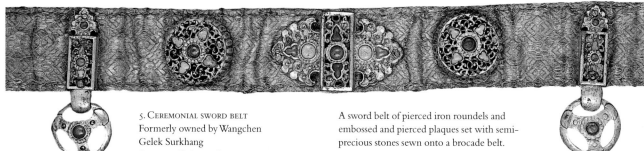

5. Ceremonial sword belt
Formerly owned by Wangchen
Gelek Surkhang
Copper-gilt, iron-gilt, turquoise,
coral, lapis lazuli and Chinese
brocade
Eastern Tibet or China,
*c*.18th or 19th century
98.5 cm long

A sword belt of pierced iron roundels and
embossed and pierced plaques set with semi-
precious stones sewn onto a brocade belt.
Two wheel-shaped hanging roundels are
suspended from the lower edge for attaching
a sword and knife. A high-quality piece
befitting an official who became one of the
four 'Shapés' or cabinet ministers of the
central Lhasa government.
Ashmolean Museum, Oxford

same basic type. Either sex wore square, rectangular and round *gau's* and small shrine-shaped *ga'us* around the neck. When a similar form of earring was worn as in eastern Tibet, the women's versions were usually larger, more elaborate and decorative and women wore pairs while men wore a single piece. Although there were a number of ornaments worn by both sexes, a larger volume of jewellery and ornament was (and still is) differentiated by gender. Men never wear bracelets or traditionally feminine materials such as pearls, conch shell or precious stones. The form and decoration of male and female amulet cases is also often different, with women's generally showing the greatest variety of geometric shapes ranging from simple round and square designs to ovals, rectangles, double-ogee-ended rectangles to octagons and cylinders. A favoured shape worn almost only by men was the large version of the shrine-shaped oblong box, with an ogival top standing to over 35 centimetres in height called *ga'u dawang* or *drepang* in central Tibet.[11] While most women's *ga'us* retain their function as relic holders, all, without exception, have a more obvious function as pieces of jewellery than do men's and make greater use of precious or semi-precious stones in their decoration.

A woman's jewellery was often her major independent financial holding, most of which came to her at marriage. At this time a mother would hand on sets of the most important pieces to her daughter. Other gifts of jewellery and clothes were given by her new husband and family.[12] In western Tibet the new clothes and jewellery given by her parents were worn by a bride at her departure ceremony in her own family house, those given by the bridegroom's family were reserved for the wedding ceremony itself at the groom's house.[13] It is a Tibetan custom for a bride to be given a jewel, usually a turquoise, by her new family to wear on her head at marriage. At the beginning of the twentieth century in Lhasa, the stone was given by a senior servant of the bridegroom's party at the time a bride left her family home.[14] More recently a mother-in-law has been the one to welcome a new daughter by putting a turquoise on her head while others recite auspicious verses in a ceremony called *yu she*.[15] In place of a turquoise, wealthy families in the past sometimes used a jade mounted in gold and set with pearls. This jewel called *tsigyu thakpa*[16] was worn on the back of the woman's headdress in Lhasa and southern Tibet. It signified her married status but divorce could be easily carried out by a husband just by the symbolic act of plucking the stone from his wife's head.[17] It was the custom for a woman to keep all the jewellery given by her relatives if she divorced or if her husband died, but the ornaments given by her husband were kept by him or retained by his family in the case of his death.

In eastern and western Tibet, and particularly amongst the nomad populations of those areas, much of this wealth was worn in the form of ornaments or stones attached to felt that extended down a woman's back. In times of crisis, the gold or silver could be sold as scrap or in its made-up form and the stones too could be sold individually or in groups as necessary. Many Tibetan refugees kept their families for extended periods in India during the decades after 1960 by gradually selling off their family jewels one by one. In Lhasa and other towns the wealthiest women would store jewels and ornaments not in use in chests as it was only on religious festivals, at ceremonies or

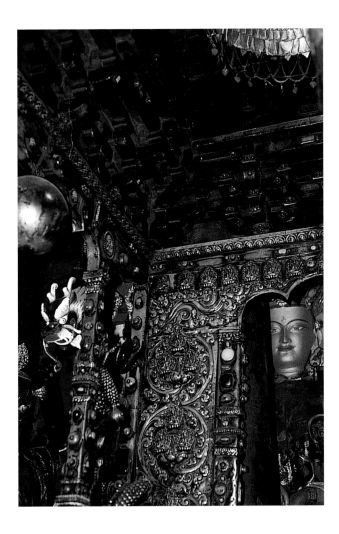

for the visits of important people that all their finery was worn.

Despite the custom of passing jewellery on in one's family, jewellery was also recycled, no longer fashionable items being melted down and the stones reused. The best gold and silver pieces, particularly *ga'us,* were alternatively given as meritorious donations to important religious figures either during their lifetime or after their death to adorn their funerary stupas or *chortens.* Giving gifts, including precious metal objects or jewellery, to monasteries or lamas was an accepted way of generating merit that was believed to lead to spiritual benefits for the individual. In Ladakh today, when a woman dies without a daughter, individual stones or even her entire turquoise-covered headdress may be given to the local monastery as an offering.[18] An early example of the practice was recorded during the journey to central Tibet of the great Indian Buddhist teacher Atisha in 1054. As the revered guru neared Lhasa, a girl who saw Atisha spontaneously gave him the ornaments on her head as an offering.[19] When new decorative *toranas* or surrounds to particularly important religious images were commissioned, it was usual to set an abundance of stones and pieces of jewellery into the metalwork as decoration. Monastic authorities could draw on existing stocks and combine them with new gifts as happened when a new screen around the Jobo, the most sacred image in Tibet, was commissioned in 1673 (plate 6).[20] The sides of the large, magnificent, gilded tomb stupas, or *chortens,* of the Dalai Lamas in the Potala Palace (plate 7) are also richly set with symmetrically arranged *ga'us*, earrings and large cut and polished semi-precious stones.

6. SCREEN AROUND THE JOBO IMAGE
Silver, corals, amber, pearls, turquoise, lapis lazuli, sapphires
Jokhang, Lhasa, 1673

The dedicatory inscription on the reverse of the silver surround to Tibet's holiest image, restored in 1673, lists as donations at the time 67 turquoises, 1,215 corals, 1,595 pearls, 4 amber teacups, 257 pieces of jade, over 3,000 precious stones, as well as numerous silver and gold rings, amulets and other ornaments. Many of these were inset into its front and sides. The inscription also gives the names of the Nepalese and Tibetan craftsmen who collaborated in its making.
Photograph Michael Henss

7. THE RELIQUARY STUPA OR CHORTEN OF THE 13TH DALAI LAMA (1876–1933)
Potala Palace, Lhasa, 1933
Gold, precious and semi-precious stones

Women's earrings and amulet boxes and the long earrings of officials are seen here set into the gilded surface of the splendid 14-metre-high reliquary *chorten* containing the body of one of Tibet's greatest recent rulers. On older *chortens* – from the first which holds the body of the 5th Dalai Lama (1617–82) to those constructed up until the mid-19th century – virtually the only jewellery items present are the large ceremonial pieces worn at the New Year.
Photograph Michael Henss

8. WOMAN FROM NORTH-EAST TIBET, 1922–40

This photograph shows the spectacular back ornaments worn in the area around the great Kokonor lake. Large dish-shaped bosses of worked silver, pieces of amber, turquoise and coral are sewn onto wide felt strips hanging from the shoulders. Such ornaments are mainly reserved for festival times today but until the 1950s were everyday wear, worn whilst carrying out daily tasks such as milking. When combined with large earrings and large round or square amulet boxes hung from their necks women could be heard coming from a distance through the clanking of their jewellery.[5]
The Collection of the Newark Museum. Gift of the Reverend Marion G. Griebenow, 1946.

## History, Change and Fashion

The evidence that would allow us to trace the history of Tibetan jewellery is unfortunately very fragmentary, confined to a small number of scroll and wall paintings, the accounts of earlier western visitors and a tiny number of archaeological finds. But exciting new evidence is being unearthed from burials of the royal period (the seventh to the ninth centuries) and two embossed gold earrings and parts of a silver-gilt reliquary of this period are now known.[21] It is undoubtedly the recycling of high-value precious metals that has resulted in the destruction of all but a few identifiable survivors from before the eighteenth century.

It is likely however that clues to far older patterns of jewellery wearing exist within the multiplicity of present-day or recent regional styles. This is particularly true of nomad groups and sedentary peoples in the eastern and western borderlands, areas politically marginalized by the Tibetan state since the seventeenth century. Until 1950 there were distinct generic similarities between key types of jewellery worn by nomads right across Tibet from the west to the east.[22] This was seen most strongly in the custom of nomad women wearing their wealth in the form of silver plaques, coins and shell disks sewn to felt strips which hung down the their backs. Amongst these groups this type of ornamentation was observed as early as the seventeenth century in north-east Tibet but was also found in western Tibet up until the 1940s.[23] Dressing their hair into the auspicious Buddhist number of 108 braids hanging to the waist, and attaching strings of turquoises to the front braids either side of the face, was an ancient custom that continues amongst nomad women in both eastern and western Tibet.[24] The practice may be first recorded in paintings of c.1042CE at the monastery of Tabo in Himachal Pradesh (plate 10)[25] and at Alchi (Ladakh) in the twelfth century.[26] It was first observed by Friar Odoric who travelled through Tibet in the fourteenth century.[27] Although the number of tiny plaits may fall short of the sacred 108, the fashion is still found virtually everywhere except in central Tibet. Another shared trait is the wearing of distinctive gold, copper-gilt or silver concave disks on their heads by women both in the western Himalayan districts of Lahaul and Spiti and in Derge and Chamdo in the east (plates 79, 80). In both areas these saucer-shaped plates are set with a central turquoise or coral.[28] This fashion was also seen in *Lh' ari* in southern Tibet until the end of the nineteenth century.[29] In all these cases we may be seeing survivals of what were probably widespread ancient Tibetan jewellery customs perhaps displaced or changed in central

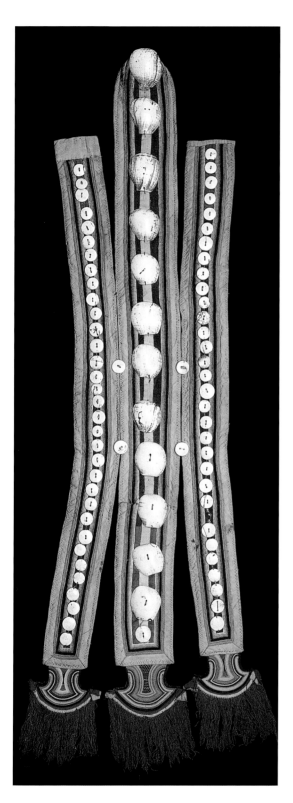

**9. WOMAN'S BACK ORNAMENTS**
Padded cotton, conch shell
North-east Tibet
Hair bags: 105 cm long, 15 cm wide
Back ornaments, middle band: 150
cm long, 37 cm wide

These multi-coloured felt strips
covered with sewn on conch shell
disks are one of the typical back
ornaments of nomad women in
north-east Tibet. The upper surfaces
of the three panels of padded cotton
are lined with variously coloured
cloths and covered with sewn on
shell disks which would reach
almost to the ground behind their
wearer. The varicoloured ends made
of cotton and velvet embroidered
with silk and gold thread decorate
the front ends of useful hair bags
concealed behind them. The full set
of ornaments also includes two
more similar felt strips which are
worn one at each side (not shown).
National Museums of Scotland

**10. MANUSCRIPT PAGE**
Tabo 'Kanjur' gouache on paper
Tabo, Himachal Pradesh, late 11th
century
A group of women kneel before a
preaching Bodhisattva. The front
braids of their hair are decorated
with lines of turquoises and large
turquoises are hung over their
foreheads, reminiscent of the
arrangement at the front of *perak*
headdresses in Ladakh today.
Photograph by Deborah Klimburg-
Salter. Western Himalayas Archive,
Vienna

Tibet by the upheavals caused by the establishment of the Dalai Lama's government from the seventeenth century onwards.

At the time of the New Year, officials in Lhasa wore exceptional jewellery and *gyaluche* costumes, the 'garments of royalty' which were said to copy those of the royal princes of ancient Tibet (plate 11).[30] Although the *ringyen*[31] or 'ancient ornaments', which survive today mostly in the storerooms of the Potala, appear to be seventeenth century or later they may copy or incorporate stones from much earlier pieces. The practice of wearing these ornaments was introduced by the fifth Dalai Lama in 1672 and was part of the ceremonial intended to evoke the splendour of the ancient 'Religious Kings' of the seventh to the ninth centuries as well as to draw a conscious parallel between his own dual secular and religious powers and theirs.[32] But the 'Great Fifth' had, in reality, both borrowed the practice from Changchub Gyaltsen (1302-64) the former ruler of Tibet and seized the jewels from his palace.[33] A very large turquoise-covered *ga'u* worn in a mid-fifteenth century *tangka,* or scroll painting, by a high official of

Drakpa Gyaltsen (1374-1432), a descendant of Changchub Gyaltsen, is almost identical to *ga'u* in the existing *ringyen*.[34]

Only a few Tibetan jewellery types, such as the round-hooped earring or *along* (plate 12) worn from at least the fourteenth century,[35] can be traced any distance back in time through depictions in art works. A mandalic amulet design has been excavated from a tomb of the eight/ninth century in north-east Tibet although as yet no portable containers have been recovered.[36] But the *ga'u* is certainly an ancient type, one of whose possible prototypes in the form of small, round amulet boxes appears in north and east Indian stone sculpture of the Pala Dynasty (tenth to twelfth centuries).[37] The strong and deep-rooted amuletic tradition of India together with the close religious connections existing between the two Buddhist cultures during the eighth to the thirteenth centuries make it likely that the custom derives from there. The image of the *ga'u* also occurs in the Prajnaparamita Sutra, an Indian scripture forming the doctrinal foundation of Buddhism in Tibet whose two earliest translations into Tibetan were in the ninth and eleventh centuries.[38] A very few, tiny, complete bronze-cast *ga'us*

11. THREE OFFICIALS WEARING THE ORNAMENTS OF THE ANCIENT KINGS, *ringyen*
Lhasa, 1937

Adorning the New Year costumes were pieces of special jewellery, the *ringyen*[6] or ornaments of the ancient kings said to date from the period of the Tibetan monarchy (7th to 9th centuries). These consisted of large, circular, gold amulet boxes studded with turquoise,[7] heavy pendant-turquoise earrings[8] and a long gold strip covered with turquoises attached to the left ear, always shown supported as here in the hand. Necklaces of large coral beads and even larger amber beads, some the size of golf balls, completed the ensemble.
Photograph by Frederick Spencer Chapman. Pitt Rivers Museum, University of Oxford

12. MANUSCRIPT PAGE
Five Hymns to the Pancaraksha Goddesses
and the Mahasannipataratnaketudharani
Gouache on paper
Dolpo, northern Nepal, c.14th century
Page size: 65 cm long, 21 cm wide

A group of donors and lama wearing the
costume and jewellery of this part of
western Tibet during the 14th century.
The first layman to the right of the
officiating lama wears earrings consisting
of three turquoise-covered drops, the third
from the lama, a woman, two prominent
gold-hoop earrings and a round convex
gold and turquoise head ornament.
The other men all wear large pieces of
turquoise in their hair above the ears.
Private collection

may date from between the seventh and thirteenth centuries; these form part of the category of small metal objects that are found in the fields called *thok cha*, or 'thunder iron', believed by Tibetans to be made when lightening strikes the ground.[39]

What little evidence we have suggests that up until the start of the twentieth century changes in the style of jewellery and the manner in which it was worn occurred relatively slowly. As the century advanced however, contacts with western culture, increasing tourism and political upheavals have had a significant impact on the role of jewellery. One of the clearest changes has been the reduction in the amount of jewellery worn on a daily basis. This trend was already visible in central Tibet before the Chinese takeover and Cultural Revolution. At the beginning of the twentieth century the Lhasa headdress or *patruk* was worn in everyday life but, after about 1930, together with other ornaments it gradually came to be worn less and less[40] and was eventually reserved only for ceremonial occasions. During the second half of the century the same trend has become more marked both throughout Tibet and the whole Himalayan region. Now, although women in the remote Zanskar Valley of Ladakh still wear their turquoise-laden *parak* headdresses even while working in the fields, this custom has entirely ceased in the Indus Valley around Leh, the capital, where tourism, film, video and television have dramatically changed cultural norms. During the last 15 years, the wearing of full sets of ornaments and headdresses has declined even at festivals in Ladakh although they are worn on official occasions and by Buddhist brides.[41] The sizes of jewellery and ornament have also changed noticeably over the

last century. Anecdotal evidence suggests that during the first half of the century there had been an increase in size and elaboration. According to Dorje Yudon Yuthok all the main female ornaments such as the *akor* had been much smaller until the early nineteenth century.[42] She believed that by the mid-twentieth century they were nearly twice the size of the earlier pieces. However, since the 1960s the trend has been towards wearing smaller as well as fewer pieces of jewellery.

While such changes in style seem to have happened gradually, the political upheavals following the Tibetan revolt against Chinese forces in 1959 and after that the Cultural Revolution (1966-77) have permanently changed Tibetan culture and transformed what people wear. After the Chinese had taken control, there was a period prior to the Cultural Revolution when many valuable objects were appropriated by Chinese officials and family jewels and religious objects were forcibly confiscated. During the Cultural Revolution there was systematic and organized looting of precious stones and metals from the religious images in monasteries, prior to their destruction.[43] The wearing of traditional ornaments was forbidden as one of the 'Four Olds' and goldsmiths and silversmiths became political targets as they not only produced religious objects but also worked for the nobility. At this desperate time some people buried their ornaments and religious objects. Only after 1980 when new laws relaxed the most severe policies of the past 14 years were people allowed to wear traditional jewellery again. What is worn today in central and southern Tibet is however a much scaled-down and much poorer version of what was worn before 1959. The

13. Amulet box, *ga'u*
Iron gilded
Eastern Tibet, *c.*15th century
9.30 cm long, 9.20 cm wide, 3.50 cm deep.

The style and extremely high quality of the pierced and inlaid ironwork on this *ga'u* link it to a well-known group of ritual objects made during the reign of the Chinese emperor Yong Lo (1403-24) which were Imperial gifts to important Tibetan religious figures. The characteristic scrollwork with lotus blossoms, which covers the front, and the signature inlaid spiral scrollwork in gold wire, found on the hinges of this exquisite *ga'u*, also suggest the same date and place of production. It may be that objects such as this formed smaller diplomatic gifts made at the time. The reverse of the box is covered with inlaid geometric ornament.
© Copyright The British Museum

few pre-1959 *patruks, ga'us* and other ornaments to have survived are now worn only at festivals. At the same time, older jewellery is frequently sold to Nepalese dealers who take it to Kathmandu while new Nepalese-made 'Tibetan' items are sold to Tibetan women who pass them on to tourists as family heirlooms.[44] But in eastern and north-eastern Tibet much more traditional jewellery is worn although it is produced increasingly by Chinese silversmiths (pages 46–9).

Within the underlying homogeneity of Tibetan culture, spanning the area from Ladakh and the Himalayas in the west to the grasslands of Qinghai province in the north-east, myriad variations existed in material culture and language, some obvious and others much more subtle. As we shall see there were strong regional preferences for particular types of amulets, earrings and belt ornaments. But most obvious of all were the strikingly distinctive types of women's headdresses, whose style and shape changed dramatically every few hundred kilometres as one traversed the Tibetan plateau from west to east.

As we have seen, the jewellery of the Lhasa nobility acted very much as indicators of rank and status both amongst male government officials and their wives. In Tsang, southern Tibet, women wore the equivalent to the Lhasa *patruk*, a dramatic D-shaped headdress called *pagor* covered in pearls, turquoises and corals. To the south-west in the Himalayan borderlands such

as Lahaul and Kinnaur, mixed populations of Tibetan and Indian peoples have given rise to the interesting mixture of jewellery types where Indian Hindu anklets, nose rings, earrings and forehead ornaments with multiple hanging drops are worn with Tibetan ornaments and some unique local pieces. In Kinnaur, Lahaul and Spiti large, oblong, lobed-ended *ga'us* called *tungma* and heavy bracelets are worn with lozenge-shaped cloak clasps and the large and unique local dress pins of brass or silver (plate 93).

Culturally Ladakh is part of western Tibet and its jewellery tends to be predominantly variants of types worn there. Women's ornaments are dominated by the striking turquoise-covered headdresses called *perak* (plates 98, 99). Stones are pierced and sewn to a tapering base of leather or felt which in the better *peraks* are over one metre long and stretch from the forehead down to the centre of the back. Recognizably different variants of the classic Ladakhi perak are found in the Zanskar and the Waka chu Valleys in Ladakh, in the Humla and Mustang districts in Nepal, in Spiti and in Ngari in western Tibet (plate 89).[45] For special occasions in Ladakh and western Tibet, freshwater-pearl earrings are combined with three or four necklaces, or *skecha*, of alternating corals, turquoises and amber or mother-of-pearl beads. Necklaces may have one or more *ga'us*, usually octagonal, at their centre. The long-standing fashion for multiple necklaces is documented by the eleventh-century murals of Tabo monastery and by fourteenth-century manuscript illustrations.[46]

Equally as rich and distinctive as the elaborate constructions of central or western Tibet are the head ornaments of women in east Tibet which tend to consist of stones tied or sewn to the hair or a felt cloth and set close to the head. Combinations of coral, turquoise and amber tend to predominate in hair ornaments and pearls are less in evidence than in central or western Tibet. From the grasslands of the Horpa (north-central Tibet) into the Chamdo and Derge areas in eastern Tibet, married women continue to wear embossed gold or copper-gilt disks, or *metog,* in their hair (plates 79, 80). The women of Gaba province on the borders of Amdo wear five or more large golf ball-sized amber balls sewn onto black felt, one at the crown of the head and others at either side, often with small corals set at their centres (plate 21). Traditional belts are of leather with attached silver plates and in both Kham and Amdo a pair of decorative belt-hangers, or *lo chab,* are suspended from belts (plates 74, 75, 76).

In the predominantly nomadic area of north-east Tibet (the former Amdo) most of a woman's ornaments are carried on her back, in the form of shell or silver bosses attached to felt strips hanging from her shoulders almost to the ground behind. At the front, from the centre of the belt, hangs an ornamental silver or brass milk-pail hook, symbolizing women's role in milking. Women from the *Gnolok* ethnic group wear equally heavy back ornaments featuring instead large amber balls into the centres of which corals are attached.

Many Khampa men today continue to wear a single plait of hair that they enlarge by entwining it with black or red threads and wrap around their head.[47] Through this they thread gold or silver rings and sometimes a plain thumb-ring of mastodon ivory. Silver clips with multiple settings of stones, or *trati,* are also fashionable. Amongst the coral- or turquoise-set gold or silver finger rings are often found 'saddle rings', or *ta gam,* so named from their shape (plate 15). A single pencil-shaped earring featuring a single coral bead similar to the type worn in pairs by women is worn in the left ear. Finely worked tinder pouches, or *mechag,* are hung from the belts of men in both Kham and Amdo and in the past it was common for men to thrust a sword, often in a turquoise- and coral-encrusted scabbard, ready for use, horizontally through their belts. In Amdo men commonly wore square or round silver *ga'u* boxes around their necks (plate 81), with large pendant or round silver earrings decorated with small corals or turquoises along their front edges.

14. WOMEN'S EARRING
Silver and coral
Eastern Tibet, *c.*19th century
15 cm long

Long earrings of this type are worn by both men and women in eastern Tibet though the presence of a decorative crescent hanger with bells suggests this belonged to a woman. Acquired in Darjeeling in 1855. V&A: 03059

15. 'SADDLE RINGS', *tagam*
Silver and coral
Central and eastern Tibet, *c.*19th century
Rings 3.5 cm long

The name of the two rings is based on their resemblance to the Tibetan saddle. They are used all over Tibet although the form originated in Kham and has remained most popular there. These were bought in 1904 in Lhasa from women selling butter in the market.
Obtained on the 1904 British Expedition to Tibet.
V&A: IM 10/11 – 1911

# Symbolism, Folklore and Beliefs

THROUGHOUT THE RELIGIONS OF THE WORLD the brilliance, beauty and rarity of gemstones have provided a metaphor for the sacred and spiritually exalted, whether embodied in an enlightened teacher, experienced in transcendent states of awareness or envisioned as paradisical landscapes. Light-saturated, jewel-like colours have also been described by mystics and by visionaries following altered states of awareness. Aldous Huxley theorized that our brains normally act as filters, allowing through only what is necessary for survival but obscuring a reality that is actually full of the intense light and colour ascribed to the heavens of the world religions and partially reproduced by the stained glass in Christian churches.[1] The paradises of cosmic Buddhas that are found in Mahayana scriptures, brought to Tibet from India, are full of descriptions of radiant colours and bejewelled landscapes. The 'Western Paradise' (S. *Sukhavati*) or the 'Land of Bliss' (T. *Dewacan*) is described in just such as manner in a first-century Sanskrit work. That world it says 'is adorned with jewel trees…the ground contains a great variety of jewels and gems… the surface of the ponds there…abound in golden water lilies, with stalks of lapis lazuli, and with shoots and stamens of diamond, well scented and delightful…'.[2] When paradises are shown in Tibetan paintings, jewels, inter-mixed with auspicious emblems, are usually painted as piles of brilliantly coloured pear-drop shapes at the bottom of the picture, where they are placed as offerings to the presiding Buddha, just as they are also shown on the upper edges of large amulet boxes.

The use of the imagery of jewels goes back to the inception of Buddhism itself in India where the 'Three Jewels' (S. *tri ratna*, T. *konchog sum*) symbol was created to represent the three pillars of the religion: the Buddha, the Buddha's teachings or Dharma and the Sangha or community of monks. In Tibet the 'Three Jewels' are shown as a pyramid with flames rising from their tops. Another symbolic jewel form the 'Wish-Granting Jewel' (S. *cintamani*, T. *yid zhin norbu*), a magical gem consisting of six or nine elongated jewels surrounded by flames, is one of the emblems most frequently found on the front of *ga'us* (plates 61, 62).[3] It was one of the 'Seven Jewels of Royal Power' (*gyaltsi rinchen nadun*) emblems of the World Ruler (S. *Chakravartin*) in ancient India. In the new Buddhist context this emblem of the power and riches of the world-ruling king became a metaphor for enlightenment's ability to satisfy all desires, both spiritual and material, with the flames blazing from it representing the radiance of the enlightened mind.[4]

The imagery of the jewel in combination with the lotus lies at the heart of the symbolism of Vajrayana Buddhism as practised in Tibet. It is famously enshrined in the Tibetan mantra to the Bodhisattva Avalokitesvara 'Om mani padme hum hri', translated as 'Hail to the jewel in the lotus'. The jewel and lotus are the two primary coefficients of enlightenment, both a description of enlightenment itself and the path to it. The lotus represents Wisdom (S. *prajna*), supreme consciousness and understanding, the container and support of all phenomena, identified with the feminine principle. The jewel is synonymous with the diamond (S. *vajra*), the active male principle of the 'Skilful Method' (S. *upaya*), the compassionate deeds which naturally arise from Wisdom. Together these qualities are the essence of Buddhahood itself. Male/female imagery runs through the whole of Tibetan religious practice expressing itself as the sexually joined images of male and female deities (*yab yum*). The jewel and the lotus thus also signify the male and female sexual organs.[5]

Some of the most renowned Buddhist teachers and religious texts have titles containing 'jewel' and 'gem' as their epithets. A famous example is the 'Jewel Ornament of Liberation or the Wish-Fulfilling Gem of the Noble Doctrine' by Gampopa, founder of the Kagyu school in Tibet (1079-1153).[6] In the Tibetan language there are several, almost interchangeable, terms that mean precious and jewel. The Tibetan word *rin chen* means 'precious' and also 'jewel', while *nor bu* translates directly as 'precious jewel'. *Rin po che* or 'precious one' is a high honorific title given to incarnate lamas although it too has the meaning of 'jewel of great value'.

In the Tibetan world there are strong beliefs in the numinous, protective power of stones to shield their wearers from harm and in their medical potency against certain diseases. Powdered stones are sometimes ground up by Tibetan doctors to form one of the ingredients in the large pills called *ril bu*. One of the most magically powerful stone beads, the etched agate *dzi*, is for example mixed with powered pearls, silver and gold dust to be taken as a remedy for epilepsy. In other preparations it dries out serum and alleviates eye diseases and fever of the bones.[7] The *dzi* is worn by both men and women to protect them from the attacks of evil spirits who can cause sickness and death. If a *dzi* breaks it is considered to have done its job of protecting its wearer but is no longer 'pure' or as effective.

16. WOMAN'S NECKLACE
*Dzi* beads, glass imitation *dzi*,
imitation jade and coral beads
Bhutan foothills, early 20th century
11.5 cm diam., largest *dzi* 3.3 cm long

This necklace is part of a complete Tibetan-style costume from the foothills of Bhutan and is typical of many in its combination of real and imitation beads. The real chalcedony *dzi* are the browner beads towards the top, the others are black and white glass imitations. Jade has been simulated by green glass while marble stained red and waxed imitates Italian coral.
V&A: IM 121–1923

Most Tibetans believe that *dzi* have a divine origin and are certainly not man made, consequently over the centuries a huge body of folklore has built up surrounding them. Some believe that *dzi* originally belonged to the gods who threw them away when even slightly blemished, a story that conveniently accounts for the many chipped and broken pieces found. Another belief relates to the legendary Tibetan folk hero Gesar of Ling who in his epic story carried off treasure from Iran, including many *dzi*, after winning a war against it. It was said that over time these prizes were dispersed all over Tibet. But the most common belief is that *dzi* are worms or insects that move under the earth and turn to stone when found by humans. In the popular imagination they are discovered in 'nests', something probably suggested by finding groups of them together. Some also believe that they must be 'fixed' or 'stopped', turned to stone by having dust thrown at them or by being spat on when they are encountered.[8]

The high Tibetan valuation of the turquoise, or *yu,* is first recorded in documents from the period of its ancient kings (seventh to ninth centuries). Contemporaneous manuscripts preserved at the central Asian oasis of Dunhuang prove it was offered in ceremonies to deities and to demons as 'ransom' in rituals to avert sickness.[9] The supernatural, the exquisitely beautiful and the precious are all variously described in Tibetan folklore as turquoise even when the colour is not directly applicable. Thus while it would be natural to describe a lake or well or some flowers as such, the epithet is also applied to the manes of horses, bees, the hair of goddesses, the 13 turquoise heavens and to the bodies of children born in a supernatural way.[10] The stone is linked, by virtue of its colour association, with Green Tara and when worshipping this deity a rosary of turquoises is ideally used (plate 17).[11] In an early twentieth-century monograph on turquoise, Tibetans were reported as valuing it second only to gold, something reflected in the way they would say 'this is turquoise and not a stone'. Big turquoises were sometimes engraved with magic formulas to enhance their power. Like prized weapons they might be also given individual names, such as 'the great star shining on the meadow land' — a stone paid as part of a tribute to the king of western Tibet in the eleventh century.[12] Fine, large stones could be given to high lamas or saints as presents while small stones, like brick tea, were once used as a type of currency.[13]

Tibetans are often experts in judging the qualities and types of turquoise and other stones. Scholars have elaborated this lore in materia medica, or medical texts, and in others which deal with the criteria by which stones and ornaments

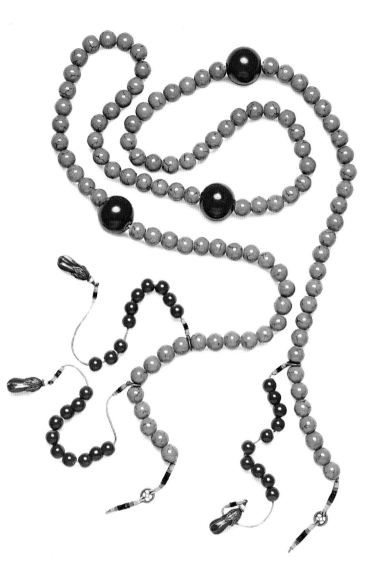

17. ROSARY, *treng wa*
Turquoise and coral
Tibet, *c.*19th century

This turquoise rosary is divided into three equal sections by three large coral beads. Three small strings of corals are added for counting the tens, hundreds and thousands of complete rosary recitations. Turquoise was considered especially appropriate for religious practice featuring the Green Tara. A similar rosary worn as a necklace may be seen in plate 64 showing a southern Tibetan woman.
© Copyright The British Museum

are judged called *dagtab*. Thus there are seven types of turquoise listed in The Blue Beryl, a medical treatise written at the end of the seventeenth century by Sangye Gyatso (1653-1705). These include red-tinted, white-tinted, superior white, refined, mediocre, blue and Chinese.[14]

Like *dzi*, turquoise has strong protective and beneficial medicinal qualities. It is believed to purify the blood and remove poison, jaundice and diseases of heat affecting the liver. It was also said that swallowing a native Tibetan turquoise was a cure for poison while to stud a *ga'u* with good turquoises was believed to strengthen the bones and prevent injury in the event of a fall.[15] The best-quality unflawed pieces are also traditionally thought to avert the evil eye, repel demons and prevent bad dreams. Another belief is that when a turquoise changes colour from blue to pale green it indicates that the wearer has an illness. While some hold that on being given to a new owner in good health its depth of colour is restored, there is also the idea that a turquoise can like a person 'die', at which point it turns green and eventually black.[16] This relates to the fact that turquoise absorbs water and, through long-term contact with the oil in human skin and exposure to light, the softer varieties tend to discolour. In a related belief, turquoises were also placed at the bottom of teacups as it was thought they would change colour if poison was present, so acting as detectors. Stones with good colour are therefore regarded as 'living' turquoise and have life-giving properties.

Coral, or *churu*, is regarded in Tibet as being lucky and power bringing for women and as strengthening the blood and aiding menstruation. It is also used in the treatment of fevers of the blood and liver or illness induced by poison. The medicinal properties of coral were known in China and integrated into the materia medica there by the Tang dynasty (seventh to tenth centuries) from where they may have spread to Tibet. Coral can represent the warmth of the sun and important symbolism surrounds its combination with the pearl, attributed to the cool moon.

Pearls in India were used as cures for eye diseases, poisoning and consumption but in Tibet are valued for enhancing women's fertility. The pearl, or *mu tig*, was linked to the moon, though black pearls were believed to relate to Saturn. As with the turquoise, The Blue Beryl text gives an extensive list of 16 types of pearls. While some of these, such as the 'inferior red pearls from the brains of Mongolian snakes' are drawn from earlier Indian mythology linking jewels to serpents or sea monster's (makara) brains,[17] others like the Chinese pearl or the pearl from the fertile regions of Amdo are likely to be

rooted in real knowledge of sources.[18] Mother-of-pearl, or *nachi*, is said to cure cough, asthma and colic and may also be used as a substitute for pearls by poorer people.[19] Like turquoise, jade, or *yangti*, was worn to forestall accidents.

Metals, like stones, are thought to possess medical properties with gold being described in The Blue Beryl as increasing longevity and dispelling demons.[20] Silver dries out serum, pus and blood while 'sweet cooling' copper dispels sicknesses of heat in the liver and lungs.[21] Iron, on the other hand, has a somewhat sinister reputation being associated with black magic and rites for casting out demons.[22]

Diamond (S. *vajra,* T. *pha lam* or *dorje phalam*) is not aesthetically prized but nevertheless plays a supreme role in Tibetan Buddhism as a symbol of the nature of enlightenment. As the clearest, hardest, most indivisible and indestructible stone known, it most naturally represents the unchanging and unbreakable brilliance and splendour of the Buddha mind. Thus the stone has both the meaning of diamond-like permanence and ultimate stability. At the same time it means 'lightning-like flash of the illumination of enlightenment'. The Sanskrit name for diamond, *vajra* (T. *dorje),* which combines all these and still further meanings, has given its name to Tibetan Buddhism itself, *Vajrayana,* 'the diamond path'.

Although much less hard (7 on the Mohr scale of hardness compared to the diamond's 10) and comparatively easily cut or broken, quartz crystal, or *man she,* nevertheless also reproduces many of the qualities of clarity of the diamond. It has also been used to symbolize the Buddha mind, particularly by the Dzogchen teachings which emphasize the pure and limitless awareness of the primordial mind within each human being. In Dzogchen initiations clear quartz in polished ball or facetted form is revealed to the student as a metaphor for this state of 'Great Perfection', which is the very meaning of the word Dzogchen. The primordial mind in a state of realized clarity, like the crystal, reflecting and refracting sunlight and creating rainbows, similarly reflects and refracts the 'rainbow' of material phenomena without becoming affected or dulled by them.

Many of these stones are used in bead form to make rosaries (S. *malas,* T. *treng wa*) whose use lies at the heart of popular religious devotion amongst monks and laymen alike. The saying of mantras or prayers is a meritorious activity believed to help offset the effects of negative deeds and generate a beneficial force in one's life. Rosaries are held wrapped around the left wrist or often are worn as a necklace, particularly in eastern Tibet (plate 77). The majority of rosaries are made from wood or seeds, with red sandalwood and the seeds of the lotus, or *rudraksha,* considered auspicious for most rites. Almost all have 108 even-sized beads, although religious texts specify varying numbers for particular practices. The number 108 has many sacred associations in Buddhism but was already a holy number in Hinduism where as a multiple of twelve and nine it represents the nine planets in the twelve houses of the zodiac.[23] Beads for counting the tens and hundreds of complete rosary recitations are added on two, small, tasselled strings of gold, silver or bronze beads (plate 17). These often have a *dorje*, representing single units, and a bell, representing tens, at their separate ends. Once one round of the rosary is completed a bead from the *dorje* string is pulled down. When ten beads have been built up on that side, a single bead on the bell side is pulled down and the *dorje* beads pushed back up. A third set of counter beads ending in a wheel or jewel for the thousands is sometimes also used. At the bottom in the centre of the rosary are three retaining beads, or *do dzin,* which symbolize the Buddhist trinity of teachings, community and the Buddha himself, here represented by the largest of the beads.

Richer members of society and high-ranking lamas were able to afford beads of precious stone such as emeralds, rubies or sapphires or, more commonly, of rock crystal, turquoise, agate, coral, pearl, amber, conch or ivory. Stones were also selected to be appropriate to a chosen deity. These included turquoise for the Green Tara, red coral or carnelian for Vajrayogini and lapis lazuli for the Medicine Buddha. But in texts different stone beads are also prescribed for use in the four main categories of rites: those of increasing, appeasing, controlling and destroying. For increasing life-span, knowledge or religious merit, the best beads are said to be of *Bodhi* or lotus seed, gold, silver, bronze or copper, while for peaceful appeasing rites, such as those for clearing away obstacles like an illness, clear or white beads made from crystal, (plate 18) pearl, mother-of-pearl, moonstone, conch shell or ivory are described as appropriate. For controlling or overcoming rites, the beads should be of coral, carnelian, red sandalwood or other fragrant substances while for rites aimed at destroying malicious spirits, beads made from *rudraksha* seeds, human or animal bone, iron or lead are advised.[24]

One of the most immediately noticeable visual aspects of depictions of Tibetan Buddhist deities is their rich adornment with gem-set jewellery. These are the 'Eight Jewel ornaments' of crown, earrings, short, medium and long necklaces, bracelets, anklets and a jewel net girdle that were derived from

the royal ornaments of ancient India. As the ideal of the Bodhisattva developed around the beginning of the Christian era, these ornaments were adopted in the religious sphere and became an essential part of the newly developing iconography. Just as the secular symbols of the universal monarch, or chakravartin, were re-interpreted by the early followers of the Buddha as symbols of his universal spiritual power, the Bodhisattva's jewel ornaments and clothes, copied from the royal costumes of ancient India, are likely to mainly symbolize spiritual wealth and power, acting as a reflection of the splendour and riches of an enlightened one's inner state.

It is, however, difficult to find any relationship between actual Tibetan jewellery and that worn by the deities of its

18. ROSARY, *treng wa*
Clear quartz crystal, turquoise, brass
Tibet, *c.*19th century
33.5 cm long

A small rosary made of clear quartz-crystal beads which, together with other white stones, texts describe as the best type for use in peaceful rites. At the bottom in the centre is a small *dorje* and three retaining beads, or *do dzin.* The saying of mantras or prayers while circumambulating religious buildings, and as part of daily devotions, is counted as meritorious. It is believed that they will help offset the effects of negative deeds and generate a beneficial force helping towards a good rebirth.
Cambridge Museum of Archaeology and Anthropology

pantheon, a situation which stands in contrast to that in the surrounding cultures of China, Nepal and India. In Tang dynasty China between the seventh and the early tenth century, courtly ladies tried to emulate the look of the Bodhisattva by wearing similar necklaces, torques and hair decorations,[25] while in Nepal key items adorning deities were worn during human initiation ceremonies up until the present. In north and north-west India depictions of jewellery on Buddhist sculptures of the first century BCE to the third century CE, and of the tenth and eleventh centuries, match either surviving jewellery or types still worn today.[26] There are some obvious cultural differences between Tibet and its neighbours that may be partly responsible for the lack of such a relationship. The close relationship between the types of jewellery worn by humans and images, reflected at life-cycle rituals in Nepal, is absent but the answer may equally lie in the very awe and veneration for such divine forms that was central to Buddhism in Tibet. Intense visualization of the appearance of a Bodhisattva or Buddha, leading to deep identification with it, lies at the heart of the Tantric path. When monk practitioners visualize themselves as deities in religious ceremonies or dances, replica ornaments and headdresses such as the 'Five Buddha' crown, or *rigna*, are certainly worn. One other ceremonial use of jewellery is the wearing of ornaments carved from human bone by monks during exorcistic dances and at other Tantric rituals. The same set of six bone ornaments are worn by wrathful guardian and semi-wrathful Tantric deities and are a condensed version of the eight ornaments worn by peaceful Bodhisattvas.[27] However, to wear the 'divine' jewellery or ornaments of deities at other times appears not to have been culturally acceptable in Tibet and might have been considered spiritually injurious.

## Emblems and decoration

Most of the symbols encountered as decoration on Tibetan jewellery were drawn either from early Indian culture or from the art of China or central Asia. Indian motifs became familiar through the importation from India of religious images, scroll paintings, books and ritual objects during the spread of Buddhist doctrines to Tibet. The borrowing of Chinese symbols probably occurred more through the importation of silks and brocades brought to Tibet by trade or as gifts and were highly prized from an early date by religious leaders and the nobility. Gifts of out-of-fashion dragon robes were also given in large quantities to important Tibetan leaders by the Chinese emperors. Amongst the borrowings from Chinese art

are the mountains, sea and clouds design and the familiar lower-hem motif from these garments, which were transferred to many contexts in the Tibetan decorative arts including the lower edge of *ga'us*. Three of the main five universal elements are shown together in this way, the rocks representing earth, the waves water and the sky and clouds air (plate 20).

Some sets of emblems such as the 'Eight Symbols of the Taoist Immortals' (C. *Ba An Xian*) have a different name in Tibet and original meanings have been lost. This set of the

19. AMULET BOX, *ga'u*
Copper and silver with inset turquoises
Probably central or southern Tibet,
*c.* first half of 19th century
10.3 cm high, 11 cm wide

The central emblem on this amulet is the powerfully protective *Namchu Wangden*, 'Sign of the All Powerful Ten', a monogram combining ten intertwined syllables in Lantsa script that together represent the elements of the universe. Each letter corresponds simultaneously to a part of the mandala of the human body and to cosmic forces. Crowning it is the sun/moon and flame symbol, *nyi da*, abbreviated here to a single flame, that symbolizes enlightenment.
V&A: 06125

attributes of the Immortals have been mistakenly interpreted by Tibetans as the Chinese version of the 'Eight Auspicious Emblems' and transliterated as *Ba shang*. In a similar way the bat (C. *fu*), whose Chinese name[28] has the same sound as the word for happiness, and is therefore a symbol for the state, loses this original meaning but retains general auspicious connotations.

It is not surprising that some of the most frequently found sets of auspicious emblems are associated with Buddhism. By far the most common set of these depicted on *ga'us*, and also the most often encountered throughout the Tibetan world, are the 'Eight Auspicious Emblems' or *Tashi tagye*. They are likely to have evolved from earlier groupings of the symbols of royalty which were appropriated and given new meanings by the emerging Buddhist and Jain religions.[29] Although the set is mentioned in early Indian Buddhist texts,[30] it is not represented in art of the same period. In fact one of its first appearances in its present form is on late ninth- and early tenth-century Buddhist drawings and silk paintings from Dunhuang in central Asia.[31] Each emblem came to symbolize an aspect of the spiritual riches and the empowerment brought to an individual by the Buddhist religion.[32] For example the Umbrella, or *dug,* an ancient Indian emblem representing royalty and dominion signifies the Buddha's universal spiritual monarchy. Another popular symbol from the set, used in its own right in Tibet as luck bringing, is the 'Endless Knot', or *pal bu,* which represents the way in which everything is interconnected and interrelated. The 'Eight Auspicious Emblems' are offered either physically or in imagined form during the consecration of statues, *rab ney,* or buildings, at the enthronement of important religious or secular persons and in a host of other ceremonies such as those intended to bless a journey.

Another ancient Indian emblem frequently found on jewellery such as *ga'us* and belt hangers (plates 20, 74) is the monster mask called *zibag,* or *tsipatar,*[33] in Tibet. Originally derived from the Indian S. *kirttimukha,* or 'Face of Glory', an emanation of Shiva found as a protection above temple doorways and religious images. In Tibet and Nepal a similar leonine face is frequently found above or below the openings on *ga'u,* guarding both the deity within and the wearer himself. In Tibet the monster mask combines the *kirttimukha's* face with the Garuda's (the half-human, half-eagle sky deity) horns, vestigial wings, its sun/moon head ornament and its two arms grasping serpents or foliage.[34] In Indian folklore Garuda represents the forces of the sun and sky who

continually wage war against the powers of the waters, represented by snakes which Garuda grasps in both arms and chews. In Tibet the Garuda, or *khyung,* was seen as a protection against poisoned water or other diseases brought by water spirits, or *lu,* and as a rain bringer through his ability to control such spirits. The many other auspicious Indian and Chinese symbols used in Tibet are summarized by Valrae Reynolds and discussed at more length by the Tibetan scholar Sherab Dagyab and by Robert Beer.

20. MAN'S AMULET BOX, *ga'u*
Silver with painted image on paper
Probably central or southern Tibet,
*c.*19th century
17 cm high, 16 cm wide

Amidst the scrollwork are the auspicious 'Seven Jewels of Royal Power', the symbolic accoutrements of the ancient Indian kings, and below them the protective monster mask, or *tsipatar,* emerging from a mountain and sea design. The flaming 'Wish Fulfilling Jewel', *yid zhin norbu,* at the apex of the box is a magical gem that brings about all desires.
Acquired during the 1904 British expedition to Lhasa. V&A: 393–906

# Metals, Gemstones, Corals and Pearls

### Semi-precious and precious stones

IN THE MID-SEVENTH CENTURY the Chinese emperor received gifts of precious stones and metals from the first great Tibetan King Srongtsen Gampo, showing that jewels were highly valued in Tibet from the very beginning of its recorded history. The annals of China during the Tang Dynasty (seventh to tenth centuries) also record that Tibetans then valued a blue stone called C. *se se*, which was probably sky-blue lapis lazuli,[1] or *vaidurya*, above all others, and that both men and women wore them as head decorations. Tibet continued to receive small amounts of lapis lazuli, used as accent points in jewellery, from the ancient mines of Badakshan, a northern province of Afghanistan, well into the twentieth century.[2]

The marked Tibetan taste for turquoise is already well documented during the period of the early Tibetan kings (627 to 836 CE). The Chinese annals describe its export at that time from Tibet while other texts list its use in ceremonies. It also took its place amongst offerings of gold, silver, gemstones, pearls and corals, piled around the bodies of the king/emperors in their tombs.[3] Further evidence for the use of pearls during those centuries comes both from archaeology and a Chinese account of the funeral practices of a people living to the north-east of central Tibet who removed their dead leaders' brains and then filled their skulls with pearls and jade.[4]

For most of its later history, coral and turquoise were the most popular ornaments in Tibet and were used everywhere, although amber and pearls were almost as highly favoured. It is hard to realistically imagine the huge quantities of coral, turquoise, amber and pearls that have found their way to the great plateau from this early period up until today. Early travellers were struck by how much was worn on a daily basis, even by poorer people. In 1775 George Bogle, envoy of the East India Company to the

Two women's necklaces, Ladakh, 19th century
upper, see plate 95; lower: V&A 03070 15

21. WOMAN WEARING GABA HEAD
ORNAMENTS
Eastern Tibet, Yushu, 2003

A festival headdress showing the
extraordinarily large amber pieces set
with corals worn in the north-easterly
part of Kham. Sewn onto felt strips
these extend most of the length of her
back. The necklaces of mixed corals
and imitation *dzi* beads are also
definitely for wear on special
occasions.

Panchen Lama at Tashilunpho, exclaimed that 'the quantity of
the first two kinds of beads (coral and amber) that is on the
head, even of a peasant's wife or daughter, is amazing'.[5] Bogle
also remarked on amber beads as big as hen's eggs, an
observation borne out by similar-sized pieces still worn on the
festival headdresses of women today in eastern Tibet (plate 21).
The enormous demand for stones was fuelled not only by
their use in jewellery and personal ornaments, such as belts and
tinder pouches, but it was also common to inset coral and
turquoise on a wide range of domestic and ritual vessels and
the sheaths of prized swords. We also know that by the early
ninth century the technique of embellishing metal images
with stones had been introduced from Nepal or India.[6] The
gold-covered and richly jewel-set images and reliquaries, or
*chortens*, that survive in Tibet's largest monasteries bear witness
to a people's deep devotion expressed through jewelled
splendour. The former wealth of its monasteries can still be
glimpsed today in images such as the 26-metre-high, gilded-
copper Maitreya, the Buddha of the future at Tashilunpho
monastery, whose crown and ear ornaments are thickly set
with gems. Even the wisdom point, or S.*urna*, between the
eyes, hardly visible from the ground, is set with a total of thirty-
one diamonds, including one of walnut size, over three
hundred pearls and more than a thousand polished pieces of
coral, amber and turquoise. For many centuries, the most
revered religious images in Tibet have also been honoured by
being further adorned with gem-set jewellery in the form of
separate breastplates, earrings and necklaces of semi-precious
stones.[7] As donations were given they became ever more
heavily and elaborately decorated. In the case of the holiest
image in Tibet, the seventh-century Sakyamuni Buddha in the
Lhasa Jokhang, successive pious gifts had, by the 1950s, covered
its entire front with a layer of jewellery (plate 1).

In Tibet the turquoise, or *yu*, has long been the most
favoured stone, valued almost as if it were on the level of a
precious gem.[8] It varied in colour and composition according
to its source being both found inside the country and
imported from China and Iran. Early documents dating to the
ninth/tenth centuries show that by then Tibetans were aware
of a number of sources of the stone within Tibet itself.
Turquoises are listed as coming from Kongpo (south-east
Tibet), and from Dargyal, a title given at that time to the
people of north-east Tibet.[9] Small deposits of turquoise
certainly exist in eastern Tibet (plate 22) and, according to a
Chinese source, near Lhasa but probably the best source of
Tibetan turquoise were the Gangchen mountains of Nari in

22. TIBETAN AND CHINESE TURQUOISE
Largest 3 cm long

Samples of turquoise collected by Bertold
Laufer on a trip through eastern Tibet during
1908-10 help make clear the difference
between Chinese and Tibetan turquoise. The
two pale green stones at the top are recorded as
Tibetan, perhaps from one of the eastern
Tibetan sources of Dayab, Batang, Derge or
Chamdo. The six more bluish-coloured samples
below them are from Honan in China.
Photograph by John Weinstein. Collections of
the Field Museum, Chicago.

western Tibet. This was the area ruled by the kings of Guge who paid a regular tribute in the stone to the kings of Ladakh.[10] Tibetan turquoise tends to be greenish and have brown or black veins, often in a spider's web pattern. Although Tibetan turquoises were prized for their magical and medicinal properties, a much higher value was given to the deep blue, flawless turquoises coming from Iran. Generally the greener and lighter a stone the less value it had. The mines of the province of Sistan in south-east Iran were one of the main sources during the nineteenth century, the stones were imported through central Asia and via Ladakh into Tibet.[11] But the most famous source, known for the quality of its stones since Roman times, lay near Nishapur in the Iranian province of Khorasan. The mines there continued to be a source for Tibet into the early twentieth century.[12]

Leh in Ladakh acted as an entrepôt centre for this trade and large quantities of Iranian turquoise passed through it to Lhasa and central Tibet. In the mid-nineteenth century many polished stones travelled in boxed drawers, each box holding 800 to 1,000 stones.[13] From the nineteenth century onwards a seaborne trade in Iranian turquoises became increasingly important, with Bombay and Calcutta as the main ports of entry to India.[14] Chinese turquoise was also brought to Tibet, perhaps from the mines of Yunnan or Hubei provinces which were operating from the start of the fourteenth century, although by the nineteenth century supplies came from Honan (plate 22).[15]

The other favourite Tibetan decorative 'stone' is red coral, *Corallium rubrum*, which is actually the calcareous exo-skeleton secreted by colonies of tiny sea animals called coelenterates. The main source of coral, or *churu*, lay far off in Italy making it even more expensive than turquoise and in 1904 a British officer found it selling for its weight in gold in Lhasa.[16] Marco Polo records the first-known use of coral in Tibetan women's jewellery in the thirteenth century, commenting that it 'is very expensive for they use it to adorn the necks of their women and of their idols'.[17] From this time right up until the twentieth century, Italy remained one of the most important sources of coral for both Tibet and Mongolia; the Tibetans particularly valuing the deep blood-red colour of Italian coral. Medieval records show that from the thirteenth century Italian merchants were supplying coral and amber to both Mongolia and Tibet. Routes began at the main coral-exporting ports of Marseilles, Livorno, Genoa and Naples. A southerly route to Tibet was used between the thirteenth and the sixteenth centuries which lay across the Mediterranean, through Syria,

Iraq and Iran, then running via Samarkand it crossed central Asia reaching Leh and finally Lhasa.[18] Small quantities of Mediterranean coral, together with Chinese and Persian Gulf coral continued to reach Tibet via this central Asian route down to the end of the nineteenth century.[19]

It was, however, the discovery of the direct sea route to India at the end of the fifteenth century that opened the way to large-scale seaborne importation of Mediterranean coral by the Portuguese and the English from the sixteenth century onwards. By the nineteenth century, Calcutta and Bombay[20] had became the main ports of entry and in the twentieth century Tibetan merchants travelled to Calcutta to buy coral at its annual fairs which featured Italian boats laden with the cargo.[21] In north-east Tibet in the late 1940s one western traveller found the pink Taiwanese and red Italian coral vying for favour and Chinese merchants conducting a direct trade in Chinese coral with the nomads of this area.[22] Today coral from Taiwan is sold in large quantities in east and north-east Tibet.

Amber, or *poshe*, the yellow or red fossilized tree resin was almost as popular as coral in Tibet and had sources on the Baltic coasts of northern Europe, Burma and Siberia. A muddy red-brown or yellow variety called Burmite was named after its source in Myanmar (Burma) and was traded to Sikkim and eastern Tibet.[23] From the early seventeenth century, the more distant Baltic amber was also brought to Indian ports by European trading companies. In the mid-seventeenth century we also have a report of Armenians trading amber carvings produced in Gdansk (former Danzig) to Tibet.[24] At this time merchants from Bhutan and Tibet also came down to Patna and Dacca (northern India and modern Bangladesh) to exchange their musk for yellow amber (and coral) beads.[25] Other supplies of Siberian amber, from the shores of Lake Baikal in Buriatia, part of eastern Siberia lying on the borders of Outer Mongolia, were being used by the nomads of north-east Tibet in the 1940s.[26] Pale yellow Russian amber which may be from the same source is being imported into eastern Tibet today.

Large quantities of both marine and freshwater cultured pearls have been used in Tibet since at least the eighth century. Although little is known about the trade in pearls before the sixteenth century, two of the main sources of supply until then, the Persian Gulf and the waters between Sri Lanka and southern India, had been fished since remote antiquity.[27] The oyster beds off the island of Bahrein in the Persian Gulf were the source of best-quality large pearls called Basra pearls. From across the Indian Ocean, pearls fished in the Persian Gulf and

the Red Sea joined others from southern India and Sri Lanka at the largest Indian pearl markets of Calcutta and Bombay, pre-eminent from the eighteenth century onwards.[28]

One little-known way in which sea pearls reached Tibet in the eighteenth and early nineteenth centuries was through the trading activities of Hindu mendicant ascetics or Gosains. These Hindu monks combined pilgrimages to holy places in India, Nepal and Tibet with a trade in gemstones, corals and pearls which they concealed in their hair or wound into their waist-cloths. We know from an inscription on an eighteenth-century Indian painting that they travelled each year to the south-east coast of India to buy corals and pearls which they traded in the foothills of Nepal.[29] Gosains travelled in large numbers to southern Tibet and 300 were noticed at Tashilunpho in 1774 by George Bogle while on the first British diplomatic mission to Tibet. He tells us that they were fed and housed by the third Panchen Lama who with his extensive trading interests was happy to support them.[30]

While sea pearls have always had their place in Tibetan jewellery, freshwater and freshwater cultured pearls have if anything been more important. Freshwater pearls from Russia were exported in the nineteenth century through central Asia to markets in Leh and Lhasa.[31] These could have come from Lake Baikal in Buriatia, said to contain large but poor-quality pearls.[32] At the end of the eighteenth century, Kalmuck Mongols living in eastern Turkestan and the lower Volga were the main pilgrim traders in Russian pearls to central Tibet. Freshwater Chinese pearls from sources in Litang, eastern Tibet, the rivers of Shensi in northern China and the Sungari River (Song Hua Jiang) in Manchuria may also have supplied Tibet.[33] From the mid-twentieth century small irregular *keshi* or 'rice crispie' freshwater cultured pearls cultivated in Japan began to oust the Basra sea pearls in Ladakh (plate 98).[34]

Another significant maritime product for the Tibetans was the conch, *Turbinella pyrum*, used in Buddhist monasteries in a

24. PAIR OF WOMEN'S EARRINGS
Silver and imitation coral
Min Jiang Valley, eastern Tibet
(border of Sichuan and Gansu), c.1970–80
15 cm long

A variant of the more usual eastern Tibetan earring
with multiple silver hanging chains and coral and
silver pendant terminals. The triple setting of
imitation corals faced forward when worn.
© Copyright The British Museum

23. PAIR OF CONCH SHELL BRACELETS, *tunglak*
Ladakh, early 1930s

Two sawn-off sections of conch shell forming simple
bracelets for women. Although no longer worn in
Tibet, the custom of wearing them continues in
country areas of Ladakh.
V&A: IS 17–1989 b&c (part of set shown in plate 97)

whole form as a trumpet or cut into round sections as bracelets (plate 23). The conch occurs in the same Indian waters as pearls especially off the coast of south-east India and northern Sri Lanka. Accounts from the sixth century onwards speak of the sea trade in shells to Bengal (now Bangladesh) where they were cut and shaped into bangles at Dacca and other centres. During the nineteenth century almost the entire output from there was sent to Tibet.[35]

So great was the demand for coral and turquoise and so potentially profitable the market that imitation stones had already begun to be made by the nineteenth century. These included glass imitation corals from Japan and China and copies of dyed bone or shell; the bulk of modern copies are made from glass or plastics.[36] Turquoise beads were faked in plastic and glass in India, Nepal, China and Japan and today dyed turquoise matrix floods eastern Tibet (plate 80). Copies tend to be slightly too glossy and of an unnaturally lurid blue or are too regular and obviously mould formed.

Although the taste for diamonds and other precious stones such as sapphires and emeralds was largely a twentieth-century phenomenon in Tibet, they were also imported earlier. A record from the end of the eighteenth century shows that diamonds, emeralds and sapphires were being imported then from India.[37] The diamonds used in Tibet at that time may have been either Indian or Brazilian but by the twentieth century are likely to have come from South Africa whose deposits were discovered in the early 1860s. Emeralds,[38] or *margad*, a form of beryl, were traded to India and Iran in large quantities from the Mexican, Peruvian and Columbian sources by the eighteenth century. The Spanish, whose conquests in the sixteenth century had opened these countries, exported their surplus stones to Goa and Diu from where they were sold on throughout India. Other supplies entered through the seaports of Bengal during the late sixteenth century.[39] Sapphire, or S.*indranila*, and rubies, or *pemaraga*, were mined in Sri Lanka although other supplies of ruby also came from Myanmar (Burma).[40] But most of the 'rubies' used in Tibetan jewellery were actually rose-pink spinels commonly called 'Balas rubies' from Badakshan (plates 110, 112). Their name is a shortened form of balakshan an Arab derivation of Badakshan. The Badakshan mines are recorded by tenth-century Arab writers and continued to supply Tibet right up until the early twentieth century.[41] Other semi-precious hardstones whose source lay mainly in Sri Lanka include pink or white tourmaline, called *amatasi* or *stang zil*, topaz and zircon. In Lhasa it was also possible to buy costly jade from the mines of Khotan in central Asia and this sometimes appears in jewellery.[42]

The trade in gemstones, coral and pearls formed a mainstay of the long-distance trade in luxury goods of high value and low weight. Merchants specializing in such trade who were resident in Tibet included Kashmiris, Armenians, Muslim Ladakhis, Chinese and Nepalese. Before the Chinese closed the border to foreigners at the end of the eighteenth century, these expatriate communities gave Lhasa a distinctively cosmopolitan feel. Of this group the Nepalese were probably the most important dealers in gems in Lhasa, the centre of the gem and gold trade. Here they owned many of the shops close to the Barkhor market surrounding the Jokhang in the heart of the old city.[43] As well as specialized traders, there were always the countless pilgrims, such as Tibetans who visited the holy sites of the Kathmandu Valley each winter and who used the opportunity to buy turquoise, agates and precious stones.[44]

## The supply of precious metals

That Tibet is a country rich in gold is evident from its early history. Tribute gifts sent to the Chinese emperors by Tibetan king/emperors between the seventh and ninth centuries include sumptuous vessels such as a wine jug in the form of a goose over two metres tall, a suit of golden armour and a complete miniature city.[45]

Not only did Tibet excel in goldsmithing at this early date but gold formed one of its leading exports, reaching the west via the Arab Caliphate and going to Tang China. It was to remain one of the foremost Tibetan exports until the twentieth century. Almost all the gold in Tibet has been extracted from alluvial or placer deposits as dust and nuggets. The comparative lack of organized mining in Tibet, and certainly of deep mining, has been the result of the strongly held Tibetan belief that mining is offensive to the earth spirits who, if angry, send illness, crop failures and other misfortune. From as early as the thirteenth century, travellers to Tibet also observed that the Tibetans often left nuggets *in situ* or replaced them when found, as they believed these, together with the veins themselves, to be somehow the 'parents' of the dust. But despite such disruptions and deep-seated religious misgivings both open-cast mining and panning has been carried out in Tibet for centuries. Gold was extracted by shovelling mud and sand into a wooden trough or artificially created stone channel. Pieces of rough woollen cloth or several short turfs at its lower end acted as strainers. As the diverted stream flowed over the sods with river mud piled on top of them, the heavier gold was freed by the running water and caught in the turf.[46]

Although gold is recorded in other areas, none of the deposits are as rich and extensive as those in the west and east of the country. In the former kingdom of Guge (western Tibet) royal annals reveal a minister in the late eleventh century with the title 'Lord of Gold', suggesting that he had been appointed to supervize extraction of gold in the region.[47] *Thog ja lung*, the most important western Tibetan mine, was still being worked in the twentieth century. At the western goldfields labour was mostly seasonal and migrant, winter working conditions being particularly harsh at the highest fields which reached an altitude of 5,000 metres. To bad weather was added the hazard of untrustworthy and even dangerous fellow workers giving something of a Klondike feel to the encampments. As one Tibetan in the twentieth century put it, 'those who went gold mining made their wills first'.[48] Most workings came under the jurisdiction of Lhasa-based *Serpons*, officials who sold concessions and extracted dues.[49]

Alluvial gold was abundant everywhere in the river gravels of eastern Tibet, east of the Yangtse. In the early twentieth century some of the richest mines were at Gyalrong, Nyarong and Erkhai and at Taining north of Dartsendo.[50] The nomads of Amdo, north-east Tibet, felt a deep unwillingness to disturb the spirits of the ground by mining and some communities prohibited any extraction on pain of severe penalties. Nevertheless gold mining was a frequent, though minor, nomad activity, perhaps encouraged by tax requirements in the form of gold dust. The richness of deposits in Amdo also attracted large numbers of seasonal Chinese miners from bordering Sichuan although the government had to protect them from attacks by religiously minded nomads.[51]

While gold was always the most valued metal, the bulk of Tibetan jewellery is actually made of silver. Although silver ore has been mined in eastern Tibet since at least the eighteenth century[52] by far the greatest supplier was China. Chinese bullion in the form of boat-shaped ingots reached Leh and Lhasa via Chinese central Asia until the early twentieth century, brought back as the profit of Indian merchants from their trade there.[53] Other Chinese silver was available at the hands of Chinese traders at centres such as Kangding in Kham in the late nineteenth and twentieth centuries. Indian silver, including the Indian rupee, high in silver content, together with old and damaged items remained important sources for craftsmen during most of the last two centuries.[54]

Any discussion of the supply of metals and stones to Tibet cannot ignore that most highly prized Tibetan bead, the *dzi*, whose very name means 'shine, brightness, splendour'. Both inside Tibet and in the community in exile genuine *dzi* of unusual pattern continue to be valued far above any natural stone. The rarity of real as opposed to imitation *dzi* and the fact that they are objects found in fields and grasslands have led Tibetans to think of them as supernatural in origin. But as we shall see *dzi* are clearly related to a much wider group of ancient, man-made Asian beads. They are usually made from chalcedony, a quartz hardstone that includes agate and carnelian. A typical *dzi* is barrel-shaped with tapering ends and is from 2 to 6 centimetres in length. These beads have distinctive geometric and symbolic patterns created in dark lines on an artificially whitened background. The most common patterns are circles called eyes (plates 16, 25), but there are many other patterns to be found including double waves or 'tiger stripes', dog-teeth and the extremely rare swastika or *yung drung dzi*. High prices, even by western standards, are regularly paid for exceptional pieces.

The consensus of opinion is that Tibetan *dzi* are of prehistoric date and some are even reported to have been found in ancient burials together with arrowheads.[55] We know that Tibetans have valued *dzi* for centuries since textual references from the sixteenth century onwards discuss their types and values.[56] It is also highly likely that banded agates or onyx were the original inspiration for *dzi*. Although *dzi* are called 'etched' agates, that is a misnomer as they are actually stained or bleached, or a combination of the two, through an application of chemicals and heat. The bleaching of stone to create a pattern is a truly ancient technique found in the Indus Valley sites dating from 2,700 to 1,800 BCE. The Tibetan *dzi* are really part of a far larger Asian decorative tradition that embraces north India, Pakistan, Afghanistan and Iran and the same production techniques were used to decorate beads in the latter country up to the mid-seventhh century CE. However, as defined by Tibetans themselves the true *dzi* is only found in Tibet, Ladakh and Bhutan.

We have some clues to the probable production technique for making *dzi* as the bleaching of agates was still happening in Sehwan on the Indus in Pakistan in 1857. At this time, washing soda or calcium carbonate in a water solution was drawn onto a carnelian plaque with a reed pen. When dry the stone was buried in the embers of a fire and left for five minutes. [57] Then when cool it was polished leaving a white design on the red stone. The whitening is not a mere surface decoration but a deep-seated bleaching of the body of the stone that leaves the surface untouched. What has just been described is a simple bleaching of a linear pattern onto natural stone but many *dzi* are produced by a combination of both staining and bleaching. A dark brown or black stain may be given to chalcedony beads by soaking them in a sugar solution, drying them and then heating them. The sugar carbonizes and changes the stone to a permanent darker hue. The bleaching technique can then be used to create light patterns on the new dark surface.[58]

*Dzi,* which have always been much sought after, have probably been imitated from an early date as the finding of copies of *dzi* in Tang period graves in China suggests. Copies were probably also made in India, Japan and Germany in a wide variety of materials including serpentine, glass, plastic and porcelain (plates 16, 25). Describing such imitations, an article published in 1932 commented that they are very common 'and can be bought in the bazaars anywhere, even Calcutta'.[59] Convincing glass copies are now entering Tibet from Taiwan.

25. NECKLACE OF IMITATION GLASS *dzi* BEADS coral and rock crystal
Tibet, *c.*19th century
36 cm long

The *dzi* shown here are mostly of the common two- or three-'eyed' type. Broken *dzi* are less valuable than whole ones and some believe that they represent beads that have protected their wearers by absorbing negative forces which have caused them to break. Pitt Rivers Museum, University of Oxford

# Craftsmen and their Work

Today, as in past centuries, jewellery production in Tibet and the Himalayas lies in the hands of two types of craftsmen, part-time country village blacksmiths and silversmiths and full-time gold and silversmiths in towns. In small villages it is common to find farmers who are also part-time metalworkers. At times of the year when there are few agricultural demands, particularly in the winter, there is an almost unbroken stretch of up to six months when metal can be worked and skills developed. *Garra,* or part-time blacksmiths, in Tibet and the Himalayan districts of Ladakh, Lahaul and Spiti meet part of the local demand for gold and silver jewellery although they spend far more time making iron agricultural tools and other copper and brass utensils.[1] But there are also many farmer/silversmiths who, especially in eastern Tibet, are important producers of jewellery and ornament.

It would be wrong to conclude that these part-time workers were partially skilled for some of the highest-quality work throughout the Tibetan world, including eastern Tibet, which was renowned for its metalwork, was made under such conditions. Where there were not enough men to carry out both farming and metalworking, the women and children of the family did the farm work or hired help might be brought in for heavy tasks. Sometimes the situation was easier and silversmiths worked within extended farming families with several brothers and sisters who maintained the farm, while they were able to devote themselves full time to their craft. Some of the best gold, silver, copper and ironworkers were concentrated in the Derge and Dayab districts of eastern Tibet. There the small villages of Derge Horpo, Derge Payul, Apishang and Dagyab were famous for the high quality of their gold and silver products and were the source of especially prized *gau's* and tinder pouches (plates 73, 75, 84, 86).[2] In most cases their continuing existence depended on their locations close to monasteries or trade routes that provided regular supplies of work. However, in the border regions of eastern and north-eastern Tibet, Chinese metalworkers made a large proportion of the Tibetan-style jewellery and other metalwork required. Chinese Muslim metalworkers in Xining and Sungpan sold their wares to Tibetans in border towns such as Batang and Litang, while others led a peripatetic life, wandering between nomad encampments on the grasslands of Amdo.[3] These highly skilled craftsmen, like the Nepalese in south and central Tibet, were able to convincingly imitate Tibetan style. In Bhutan, before metalworkers were centralized in Thimpu in 1952, most worked for their local district administrator, or *dzong pon,* who paid them an allowance.[4]

Although jewellery and ornaments were made by village craftsmen across Tibet and the Himalayas, the greatest numbers of full-time jewellers, or *ta zowa,* lived in major towns, a situation that continues today. The large market town of Shigatse in southern Tibet was a major centre for the production of silverwork for which it was well known. A western visitor in 1939 noticed that most of the women's jewellery produced there was made by Newar craftsmen from Nepal.[5] The same craftsmen made a large contribution to jewellery production in Lhasa (see below) and in towns and villages all over south and central Tibet.

## Gold and silversmiths in Lhasa

As the biggest centre of population the capital, Lhasa, with its constant stream of incoming pilgrims and merchants offered the largest market and was the greatest centre of jewellery production. Lhasa was renowned for its gold jewellery and one nineteenth-century western visitor commented that 'in Lhasa even the poor people wear gold jewellery'.[6] During the period 1930-59 there were around 100 jewellers, both Tibetan and Nepalese, in the capital. Of these, however, perhaps only 15 to 20 were capable of high-quality work while only a handful of about five to seven frequently worked for the nobility.[7] The commonest commissions from the officials of the government were those they required to show their status (pages 64–5) but there was also a huge production for their wives.

The continual demand for jewellery in Lhasa was not confined to the nobility, and, as almost everyone possessed at least an amulet box and a necklace, it spanned all classes. Visiting or local merchants, pilgrims from as far away as Mongolia and monks from the nearby monasteries of Ganden, Drepung and Sera could all on occasion be clients. *Geshu,* or novices up to the rank of *gelong* or ordained monks, ordered

26. THE EX-LHASA JEWELLER TSERING CHOPHEL, (B. 1921) Dharmasala, 1987

One of the best jewellers in Lhasa during the 1940s and 1950s, Tsering Chophel now works in Dharamsala, northern India, for the Tibetan community in exile. Although in Tibet he worked only on gold jewellery, today he also makes metalwork of all types, including vessels in silver.

small round *ga'us* to hold the image of their *yidam* or tutelary deities. The *khenpos*, or abbots of monasteries, also needed large shrine *ga'us* to furnish their private shrine rooms and to carry for protection on long journeys. While such orders were unofficial, the government itself sometimes needed jewellers to set stones into the sides of ritual objects, or perhaps the crown of a newly made deity being installed in one of the large monasteries surrounding Lhasa. For such work the government used jewellers from its own workshop situated just below the Potala in the village of Zhol. This building called the *Dod zhol pal khyil* housed about 150 metalworkers of all types organized into guild groups. Amongst them were about ten jewellers who worked in concert with gold, silver and coppersmiths and others.[8] When off duty, government workers were free to take private orders and were frequently commissioned by officials to make hat ornaments and other jewellery of rank for them. In Lhasa before 1959 freelance goldsmiths tended to be highly specialized and generally only worked gold and cut stones.[9]

As we have seen, the Newar craftsmen of the Kathmandu Valley were important producers of jewellery throughout central and southern Tibet and they were also amongst the most valued jewellers of the capital itself. There was probably an established colony of Nepalese traders and metalworkers in Lhasa by the late seventeenth century.[10] These were either Newars from the Kathmandu Valley or the offspring of Newar men and Tibetan women, called *katsaras*, who were prohibited from inheriting their father's wealth in Nepal and often became traders or metalworkers in Tibet. During the nineteenth and the first half of the twentieth centuries, western visitors wrote of Newar craftsmen as the most skilled metalworkers, casters and jewellers in Lhasa. Although before the late nineteenth century they had evidently been important in the government workshop, they were barred from entry to it by the 13th Dalai Lama (1876-1933) probably as part of his conscious programme to promote an independent Tibet.[11] However, Newar gold and silversmiths continued to be privately patronized by laymen and monks alike in Lhasa during the first half of the twentieth century (plates 28, 61) and continued to work in Tibet even after the Chinese invasion of 1950.[12] One of their noted skills lay as jewellers, particularly in stone setting and filigree work (see pages 60–61).[13]

In Tibet there was, and still remains, a prejudice against metalworkers of all types. This is mostly a legacy of Buddhism which has looked down on all those taking life or dealing with

27. THE EX-TIBETAN GOVERNMENT SILVERSMITH CHOGYAL, (B. 1939) AND WIFE
Gangtok, Sikkim, 2000

This craftsman worked in the Tibetan government workshop below the Potala Palace during the 1940s.

28. WOMAN'S AMULET BOX, *ga'u thubzhi*
Silver-gilt, turquoise
Lhasa, *c.* late 19th century
9 cm by 9 cm square, 2 cm deep

The accession details record that this *ga'u* was made by Newar craftsmen in Lhasa. It was probably typical of a large production commissioned by those of moderate means that both Tibetan and Newari silversmiths and jewellers were responsible for. This was the most fashionable type of women's amulet box in Lhasa during the 19th and early 20th centuries.
Bought from Annie Taylor.
National Museums of Scotland

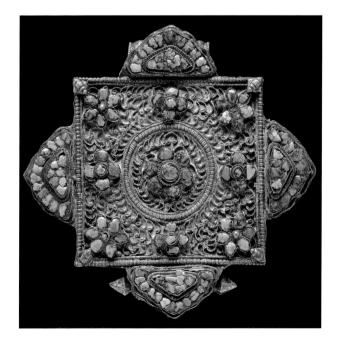

products made from dead animals such as tanners and butchers. Metalworkers and particularly ironworkers were included in this group as they made tools and weapons that either directly or indirectly took human and animal life. In spite of the general antipathy to blacksmiths, who mostly lived on the outskirts of towns and cities like Lhasa, those who made objects in the precious metals were regarded in a much better light. Both the nature of the materials themselves, and the fact that gold and silversmiths were often producing things of a religious nature, helped to raise their status in popular eyes. In Lhasa therefore there was no objection to the common practice of gold and silversmiths renting houses in the centre of the city while maintaining their main residence on the outskirts.[14] They had cellar-like, below-ground-level workshops although they would often work on the street above and have a few finished pieces at their side to attract the attention of passers by.

In contemporary Tibet with its improved communication links, there is much greater mobility of craftsmen than ever before. This has led to large numbers of metalworkers from eastern Tibet and Chinese craftsmen from Yunnan settling and working in towns throughout Tibet including Lhasa. Within the last ten years, silversmiths from Hoqing in Yunnan have settled in the towns of eastern Tibet in particular where they now dominate the production of jewellery. This has probably been achieved by their use of semi-automated methods to produce work more cheaply than local Tibetans. These pioneers were alerted to the economic possibilities in east Tibet by an earlier wave of Tibetan traders who, from the 1940s onwards, patronized them in Yunnan and found they could order cheap copies of Tibetan objects to take back to Tibet. Tibetan-style ornaments made by them are generally of poorer quality than traditional Kham pieces. However the picture is not entirely bleak for local Tibetan craftsmanship in east Tibet. Skilled part-time silver and goldsmiths still operate in the farming villages of the area and, probably because they do not have to rely on metalworking as their main income, they do not have to compete with Chinese newcomers and can continue to supply the quality end of the market.

## The ordering and making of jewellery

In the past when business was slack, jewellers might make a few pieces to sell ready-made but the bulk of their work was done on a commission basis. In common with other metalworkers, they often went to the house of a wealthy patron who was ordering a large number of pieces to make them on the spot. During the time there, from a week up to several months, they would receive a daily wage, plenty of good meals from the family and a final present.[15] While all the raw materials were available in Lhasa and craftsmen could be asked to obtain them, patrons frequently provided them in the form of scrap jewellery and recycled stones taken from redundant older pieces. Today craftsmen continue to mostly make things on commission basis. When ordering, a client might bring a model to be copied or a craftsman may sometimes draw out a design for approval.

Gold and silver are measured in Tibet and Nepal in tola weights, one tola being equal to 11.5 grams, a unit said to have derived from the weight of an old Indian silver rupee. Various recipes involving natural substances were used in the past to give different finishes to gold. A fifteenth-century text records one designed to give a patina of age that relied on a mixture of brass and copper dust, juniper seeds, iodine salt, sulphur, rock salt and burnt sugar.[16] But gold with a reddish tinge, or *ser dang*, was the most appreciated finish and a variety of methods, all non-permanent, were used to achieve this. In one, gold was first

29. FIRE OR MERCURY GILDING
Derge Peyul, eastern Tibet, 2003

In order to fire gild metal, a mixture of mercury, stone and glass particles and gold are first ground together with water in a ratio of four parts mercury to one of gold. After the metal to be gilded is cleaned in acid, it is coated with an amalgam of the ground gold and mercury. Here we see the moment that occurs after two or three minutes of heating on a brazier, when the mercury evaporates to leave a layer of pure gold. The operation is taking place in the street with onlookers at a distance as the vapour is highly poisonous.

cleaned by heating it with borax and fruit acid and then boiled with pieces of silver and copper in a solution of a colourant used in dyeing.[17] Most gold and silversmiths gild their own objects using mercury or fire gilding *tsha ser* (see plate 29 for description of the process). Although electro-plating is easier, safer and cheaper, coverage is thinner and paler in tone than the admired rich hues found on fire-gilded pieces.

In Tibet the term for goldsmith was *ser zowa*, derived from *ser* or gold and *zo* meaning 'maker'. Although there was another word for jeweller, *ta zowa* or 'stone cutter/setter', in practice goldsmiths often also cut and set stones and the terms were interchangeable. Silversmiths, or *nul zowa* 'makers of silver', were also, as we have seen, large producers of jewellery and ornament. In towns gold and silversmiths workshops usually open onto the street or are tucked behind a small shop area. Today many Chinese workers in Tibet actually live in their workshops and a tiny sofa and television may look down on the anvil and hearth. In country villages where there is more space, workshops are often close to a craftsman's house in a lean-to to give maximum light. The actual working area is usually quite tiny. A metalworker sits cross-legged behind his small mud or mud-brick hearth, usually not much more than 60 centimetres square, at one side of which is a goatskin or metal mechanical bellows. Charcoal made from willow, poplar or thorn wood smoulders at its centre ready to be blown to a red heat by the bellows. A short upright anvil will be stuck into a log close by. The hearth is essential for a variety of operations: for the melting of metal in crucibles when casting, for annealing or softening metal to prevent it becoming brittle, and for heating fluxes and solders. A nearby bowl of cold water is also needed for cooling hot metal and another holding an acid to clean the oxides and fluxes from a piece after working.[18] Although the names of tools vary slightly from area to area their forms are basically similar throughout the Tibetan world. The same can also be said of the techniques of production, many of which probably have prehistoric origins. It is only in the last few decades that technological innovations have crept in such as the use of mechanical rather than goatskin bellows, or a western-style vice for holding small pieces of silver rather than the hand-held wooden clamp, or just hands themselves.

30. JEWELLER'S WORKSHOP
Leh, Ladakh, 1986

The workshop of a Muslim jeweller in the centre of Leh showing a craftsman at work on a gold amulet box. A hearth and hand-turned mechanical bellows are situated in front of the goldsmith.

31. EMBOSSING ORNAMENTS FOR A BELT
Derge Peyul, 2003

A craftsman chases the front of an ornament set into pitch which absorbs the hammer blows. For working the back, the pitch, which lies on a wooden board, must be warmed to remove the pieces, which are then re-set. There must be no air spaces under the metal or the plaques will crack.

Chinese metalworkers are also introducing gas blowtorches and a far greater use of die stamping to speed up production but, on the whole, the ways in which pieces are made still reflect ancient traditional practices.

A large percentage of work relies on a combination of the simple raising of shapes by beating or *dungpa*, and fine embossing or *tsakpa* techniques. Embossed designs, or *bur tshag/hrob tshag*, are first raised by means of punching and then sharpened and embellished by chasing, a technique that pushes metal apart each side of the line of impact rather than removing it as in engraving. In both cases a hammer is used in conjunction with punches or chisels. In eastern Tibet where silversmiths took the most time and care over objects, an 18-centimetre-high *ga'u* box might take a month to finish. For each working the sheet metal must be set into pitch, which supports it while it is being beaten and chased. A sticky pitch, or *lam ber,* is made from a mixture of heated aromatic tree resin called *pokhar*,[19] mustard seed oil, Chinese or Indian vermilion dye and a filler such as pulped tree bark or ground clay.[20] A variety of differently sized hammers, or *tho ba,* punches, chisels, shears, files, tongs and wire brushes are used by smiths in their operations. The various sizes of punches and chasing chisels, or *zong,* used for modelling and raising have many names varying from region to region. The punches used in embossing are rounder while sharper-edged chasing chisels are employed for making fine straight lines.[21] There are a host of other punches and chisels used to make round surfaces, repeating patterns and curved lines.

A box *ga'u* in central or south Tibet is worked for a minimum of three times beginning from the front, following an initial stencilled or drawn design. It will then be embossed from the reverse and finally chased from the front. A better result is obtained by a further repetition of both processes. The main reason that craftsmen from eastern Tibet were so renowned was that they embossed *ga'us* and other pieces not three or four times as was usual elsewhere but up to as many as eight or nine times, alternating work from the back with chasing from the front to produce a pin-sharp crispness of detail (plates 84, 86). Each time the piece was removed after working, it was heated to prevent it becoming brittle, cleaned in an acid solution and then washed. In eastern Tibet each of the auspicious emblems would be embossed and gilded separately.

The extensive use of ribbed or 'pearled' wire, or *buti,* in Tibetan jewellery creates a large part of its distinctive look and feel. In a thick gage it is used to form earrings (plates 65, 66)

32. WIRE DRAWING
Chamdo, 2003

To make pearled wire a craftsman first hammers a silver ingot into a long thin rectangle and then rounds the edges. This picture shows how this is then pulled repeatedly through smaller and smaller holes in an iron plate using large pincers. After a few pullings it must be heated to prevent the metal splitting. One tola weight (11.5 grams) of silver will make up to an amazing 1,025 metres of wire.

33. SILVER GRANULATION
Chamdo, 2003

Here we see small granules of silver being set onto the side of a man's queue ring. The tiny balls must be matched in size by eye and then attached using a dab of silver/copper solder which is heated until it fuses the balls with the bezel. Granules are first made by melting small snippets of silver on a charcoal bed with a borax flux, which helps them liquify while the charcoal keeps them separate as they form.

and in thinner diameter to decorate the front edges of *ga'u* boxes, rings and many other items. To create the effect, wire is drawn repeatedly through thinner and thinner holes in an iron drawing block, or *tranyi*,[22] and then ribbed using a tool made from a block of wood with a grooved iron blade, or *booga*[23], which is rolled backwards and forwards along its length. Pearled wire is also plaited to enrich the fronts of belt hangers and head ornaments in eastern Tibet. Seams are joined and small elements such as silver granules and pearled wire attached to surfaces using solder in conjunction with a borax flux or *tsala kharpo*.[24] Borax is found on the salt lakes of the high northern Changtang and has the useful chemical action of cleaning as well as helping to prevent the oxidization caused by heating, so promoting fusion. A common solder for joining silver combines copper, zinc, tin and silver. This is placed on the join where a solution of flux has already been applied and intense heat is directed onto it by means of a thin blowpipe or, more recently, a blowtorch.

Chinese silversmiths working in Tibet at present are using production methods that cut down on the costly, time-intensive processes of embossing. Two-piece, base-metal dies, cast by the craftsmen themselves, are used to punch out belts, plates, *ga'u* fronts and other popular ornaments. A final chasing from the front is used to sharpen the indistinct struck design. The die method is mainly used for items in great demand and Yunnanese craftsmen do still make single objects. An even more recent innovation is the introduction of factory-made kaolin moulds for cheap rings, earrings and small pendants produced by a company in Fujian. These are miniature, mass-produced, lost-wax moulds which allow a complete ring or earring to be made in under ten minutes including time for cleaning and trimming. For the most part Tibetans have not as yet adopted these methods although they sometimes use two-piece sand moulds for belt hangers and *ga'u* fronts.

## Stone cutting and polishing

Tibetans may have learnt the intricate art of carving semi-precious stones from their Nepalese neighbours who lived and worked as jewellers in Tibet from at least the end of the seventeenth century and probably long before. Unfortunately Tibetan literature makes little mention of gold or silver working techniques which were generally not thought of as sufficiently important compared to religious or even medical themes.[25] But a few inquisitive scholars did record some aspects of stone cutting and metalworking within craftworking sections of larger encyclopedias of Tibetan culture. It is fascinating to find that several key techniques involved in working semi-precious stones recorded by the great fifteenth-century religious leader Ratna Lingpa (1403–73) are closely comparable to those used by craftsmen today.[26] Good-quality diamond is described by him as the best material for cutting, chopping, rubbing and piercing but, if this is not available, he says one should use a wet copper blade to pick up a crushed stone called *koranza* and then 'cut the jewel as a carpenter would cut a piece of wood'.[27] Today, turquoise, lapis lazuli or coral are cut using a strip of copper in just this way with a solution of grey abrasive corundum called *kolentsi* or just with crushed garnet. *Kolentsi*, probably the same as *koranza,* is used by present-day jewellers both as a whetstone with water to polish and shape and to make abrasive powder. Another green-grey, fine-grained sandstone called *datowoka* is used for shaping and polishing and both stones, according to informants, are found in central and southern Tibet. *Kolentsi* powder or ground glass can also be mixed with liquid pitch, or *ber,* and cast into an artificial whetstone about 15 centimetres long. The finest polishing is sometimes carried out by using a Bhutanese bamboo called *ba* that can also be cut into slivers to make thin lines on the surfaces of stones.[28] For piercing stones, Ratna Lingpa observed that a copper needle was used with more *koranza* powder and water. To make the handling involved in the process of polishing a small stone easier, the early account says it can be stuck to a support such as a stick with pitch. There were also recipes for enhancing the colour and lustre of stones just as there were for gold. Ratna Lingpa in the passage quoted above says that turquoise may be made lustrous by boiling in good-quality barley beer, or *chang,* or made golden by repeated polishing with a melted mixture of crystal, kaolin, copper, silver, lead and saltpetre.

Both technological limits and the dictates of their own taste have meant that only the softer semi-precious stones such as turquoise and lapis lazuli were cut in Tibet and, when intended for rings, are either flat or of a rounded cabouchon form. Today, as in the past, *ber*, or a substance called *lacha* made from the secretions of the insect *Laccifera lacca* and mustard oil, is used to stick stones into their bezels. Stones are simply pressed down into the hot pitch, which holds them once cool, but the method is far from effective in the long term as the pitch dries and stones often fall or are knocked out. It was said that when members of the Tibetan government were dressed in their official ornaments, they preferred to ride slower mounts such as donkeys rather than risk riding faster on horses and jogging free some of the stones they were wearing.

# Jewellery in Nepal

ALTHOUGH NEPAL IS GEOGRAPHICALLY SMALL, the equivalent of Austria and Switzerland combined (140,798 square kilometres), it contains a huge diversity of landscape and climate matched by a multiplicity of ethnic groups, languages and cultures. Surrounded by India on all but its northern border, which lies against the Tibetan Autonomous Region of China, it encompasses the greatest possible variation in altitude and corresponding climatic zones anywhere on earth. From the Terai in the south, which is only a hundred metres above sea level, the land rises to the stupendous Himalayan mountain range in the north, which includes Mount Everest, the highest point on earth at 8,848 metres. From the beginning of its civilization, Nepal's mountains, which cover 90 per cent of its area, have shaped its history and cultures. Its three main mountain chains: the Middle Hills, the Churia Range and the Himalayas have acted as a major barrier to conquerors from both Tibet in the north and India in the south. Although suffering an incursion in the medieval period, Nepal was never, for example, occupied by Muslim forces and this allowed its unique cultural blend of Hinduism and Buddhism to continue developing until the present day. The other main legacy of its mountainous topography is that throughout its history Nepal has been a place of refuge for persecuted peoples. The largest numbers have come from India but influxes of Tibetans have also had a large impact on Nepal's culture. Their presence is felt not only where it might be expected in the high Himalayan border zone but also in the Middle Hills, the heart of the country, where the ethnic Gurung, Tamang, Magar, Newar, Rai Thakali and Limbu speak Tibeto-Burman languages revealing their ancient Tibetan origins. The complexity and the richness of its present day multi-ethnic society with its 37 languages is primarily the result of this historical role as refuge zone and the blending of such peoples over more than 2,000 years. It is possible to

Ceremonial necklace from Nepal (plate 113)

broadly correlate the three main geographical divisions of the Terai, Middle Hills and Himalayan areas with cultural and ethnic groupings. These divisions run roughly parallel to the Himalayan mountain range in the north.

Much of the Nepalese jewellery in this volume was made and worn by the Newars of the Kathmandu Valley, an area which forms the historical heartland of Nepal lying at the centre of the Middle Hills. The valley is a bowl about 19 kilometres wide by 24 kilometres long surrounded by a rim of mountains, its dense population supported by a temperate climate allowing up to three crops a year. Culturally and economically it is the most important area in Nepal and contains the capital Kathmandu, seat of the government and monarchy. The Middle Hills themselves are in reality the Mahabharat Lekh mountains rising to 1,000-2,000 metres. Within the fertile valleys and terraced hill and mountain slopes of this 75-kilometre-wide zone live the majority of Nepal's estimated 21 million population. In the far south alongside the Indian border lies the Terai, a flat sub-tropical lowland. Formerly the area was a malaria-infested jungle but clearance and malaria eradication a few decades ago have turned it into the richest arable land in Nepal. In the north of the country is the Himalayan region where in the valleys, between 3,000 and 5,000 metres, live Tibetan Buddhist peoples, the Sherpa of Solu Khumbu and the people of Humla, Doplo, Mustang, Manang and the Upper Aran.

## The Newars

The Newar people may have emerged in their Kathmandu Valley homeland by as early as the sixth century BCE. They were the result of intermarriage between a group called the Kiratas, who had come from north-east India a century or so earlier, and the first settlers of the valley. The society was agriculturally based and it was to be the riches from trade and over a thousand years of royal patronage that were to fuel the well-developed Newari artistic culture. The Kathmandu Valley lay on main trade routes between India and Tibet but was also blessed with a temperate climate and flat, fertile land. Most Newars live in the Middle Hills and the valley itself where they make up more than half the population. They are an industrious people who traditionally excel as traders and craftsmen although farmers, or *Jyapu,* still form over 50 per cent of the population of the valley.[1] The Newars of today are the result of intermarriages in the distant past when Buddhist monks and Hindus fled the Muslim invasion of northern India between the twelfth and thirteenth centuries and later when Hindus escaped inter-dynastic wars and persecutions. The mix of peoples and religions has led to the development of a highly complex society whose organization was moulded by the imposition of a formal caste system by the Hindu ruler Stithimalla (r.1382–95) in the fourteenth century. Although formally abolished in 1960, the Nepalese caste system devised then, which integrated Buddhists and Hindus into a layered

34. DURBAR SQUARE, BHAKTAPUR, NEPAL, 1988

This picture shows the typical pagoda temple style of traditional Nepalese architecture with their carved wooden facades.

structure, continues to underpin Newar society.

Religion is the other great defining force for identity in Nepal. The majority of Newars follow Hinduism, with a tiny percentage being Buddhist and 3 per cent Muslim, while Christians, Jains and others account for the remainder. However, the picture is far more complex than this bare analysis alone can suggest and ignores the overlapping and syncretism that is such a strong feature of religion in the Kathmandu Valley. Perhaps the most ancient layer of religious belief, and one still much in evidence today, is that of animism which sees all natural phenomenon as alive and governed by indwelling spirits that may be benevolent or malevolent and which must be propitiated to ensure their good will. Of the main Hindu deities Shiva is the most popular, worshipped by almost all Hindu Newars in his forms as Pashupati and the fierce Bhairav. The female embodiment of Shiva, the fierce but beneficent Durga, is the most loved and worshipped goddess, shown in her most popular form riding a lion and killing the buffalo demon Mahisasura (plate 35). Buddhism, though a minority religion, continues to be of considerable importance in the Kathmandu Valley. Buddhism mainly entered the country in its Mahayana or 'Great Path' form which stressed the ideal of the Bodhisattva. As less remote beings than Buddhas, Bodhisattvas came to be worshipped and petitioned for help in human affairs and their forms multiplied over the centuries. As Buddhism evolved in Nepal, it interrelated with Hinduism producing a remarkable and generally tolerant syncretism which has led to Buddhists and Hindus worshipping the same deities, each under their own names, at many shrines. Hindus worship Buddhist gods as Hindu deities but equally Buddhists venerate Hindu deities.

The many festivals of the Newar year, honoured by Buddhist and Hindu, low and high caste alike, are spectacular religious occasions that bring all its people together. Many are *yatras* when the gods or goddesses are dressed in lavish clothing and jewellery and carried on chariots through the streets. Amongst the most important is the *yatra* of the royal Kumari in Kathmandu. The goddess Kumari is believed to incarnate in the form of a young virgin Newar girl who becomes a living goddess. Although most of the valley towns have their Kumari, the royal Kumari embodies the form of Durga called Taleju, the special protector of the royal family and the nation. Girls who are chosen for the royal Kumari must be fearless, physically unblemished and without wounds. One of the most fascinating aspects of the Kumari is that much of the jewellery she wears on ceremonial occasions is identical to that worn by

35. CEREMONIAL AMULET BOX, *jantar*
Silver-gilt, pink and blue sapphires, rubies, emeralds
Kathmandu Valley, Nepal,
*c.*19th century
11.5 cm long, 9.5 cm wide,
4 cm thick

The front of this case is embossed with probably the most popular deity in Nepal, the Goddess Durga, shown here in her eight-armed form as the destroyer of Mahisasura, the buffalo demon (Durga Mahishasuramardini). The goddess rides on her lion mount and spears the demon emerging from a buffalo to the right. A piece of such high quality bearing the nine planetary gems on its reverse may quite possibly have been worn by the goddess Kumari, one of the living incarnations of Durga.
Private collection

36. Reverse of ceremonial *jantar*,
PLATE 35
Silver-gilt, coral, pearl, garnet, emerald,
cat's eye, topaz, sapphire, ruby

The *nau ratna* or 'nine gems' which
each represent one of the visible
planets, sun, moon and two
mythological planets, Ketu and Rahu.
In India and Nepal these have been
worshipped as deities since ancient
times and are regarded by both
Buddhists and Hindus as giving
protection against misfortunes brought
by malign planetary influences. In this
case the central stone is a coral carved
in the form of Ganesh representing the
sun, although ruby usually takes this
position (and the sun is represented
again in the outer circle). Around it are
arranged in a microcosmic model of
the planetary system: the pearl
(Moon), coral (Mars), topaz (Venus),
ruby (Rahu), cat's eye (Ketu), garnet
(Sun), white sapphire (Jupiter),
emerald (Mercury) and sapphire
(Saturn).

girls during their early rites of initiation, by brides and by
women entering old age. The life of a Newar of either gender
is punctuated by ceremonies that celebrate and bless its key
stages or *samskara*.

## Newar Jewellery

Most Nepalese believe that jewellery has strong protective and
health-giving properties helping to draw beneficial energies
into the life of its wearers. Much of this power has to do with
the inherent qualities of the raw materials involved. Gold (N.
*sun*), the purest and most sacred metal since it is incorruptible
and will not pollute, is identified with the sun god Surya by
Hindus. These qualities have led it to be considered the best
material for personal ornaments, especially those worn on the
head, the purest part of the human body. In the ayurvedic
medical system followed in India and Nepal, gold is believed
to increase sexual potency and to benefit the head. Silver (N.
*chandi*) is the second ranking in purity in the Hindu world,
associated with the moon and the feminine. Even the impure
copper (N. *tama*) and iron have beneficial qualities: copper
purifies the blood and iron repels evil spirits and ghosts. The
Hindu beliefs which helped shape Kathmandu Valley society
ascribe particular protective properties to stones, corals and
pearls. Coral is associated with the planet Mars and necklaces
made from it are thought to act as an antidote to malign
planetary influences. Coral also features in the *nau ratna* or
protective 'nine gems' set which is also popular in India. The
stones are arranged in a mandalic form on rings or amulets,
with each one corresponding to one of the visible planets, the
sun and two mythological planets (plate 36).[2] Each is believed
to receive the energies of their corresponding celestial body,
deified as gods and goddesses. Set in a pendant or ring, they
protect from all bad planetary influences.

For the Newars the giving and wearing of special jewellery
helps to mark and sanctify the major stages of a person's life.
There are individual pieces and some sets of ornaments that
are worn only on particular occasions. By wearing the finest
jewellery Newars believe women bring blessings on important
occasions; in the case of marriage this beneficial power is
directed particularly towards the woman's new husband and
also strengthens prayers for fertility and wealth in the couple's
future life together. Newar women wear as much jewellery as
possible at their marriage, ideally made of the purest gold.
Although family pieces are given by a mother to her daughter
as part of her dowry, marriage is also a time when most major
new pieces are ordered by families. By tradition both the

groom's family and the bride's parents give gold and silver jewellery of a set weight, a situation that contrasts with India where the bride's family are expected to bear the whole burden of this provision.

While the preciousness of jewellery is deeply rooted in religious beliefs and the desire to draw happiness and protection into one's life, its economic value remains central. The main part of a bride's dowry is a certain quantity of gold jewellery, specified by tola weight (see page 46). This is in theory a woman's own property, one of the few sources of disposable wealth that by traditional law she can hold, being barred from inheriting property.[3] It forms a measure of financial security to be kept against the exigencies of life – sickness, old age or widowhood. However, in reality sons and husbands have access to such pieces and can pawn or sell them if the need arises. When money becomes available again, new jewellery can be ordered and restored to its wearer.

Although shadowy the early history of Nepalese jewellery is illuminated by brief but fascinating glimpses afforded by mid-seventh century Chinese visits to the kingdom. The envoy of the Chinese emperor at this time observed the Newar king Narendradeva wearing gold earrings with pendant jade drops, a belt with gold plaques ornamented with Buddha images and an array of semi-precious stones (see page 58).[4] The early Chinese visitor recorded that the common people at the time wore horn and bamboo ear ornaments which no doubt reflected their low economic status and ancient tribal preferences for natural materials.[5] Other natural substances such as seeds and teeth were also probably widely worn and their forms have survived in some cases into later centuries as pseudomorphs, copied in precious metals. The ribbed, seed-like surfaces of the *tilhari* and *nau gedi* (plate 37) beads of today suggest natural prototypes and *nau gedi* actually means 'seed' as well as 'bead'.[6] The Chinese envoy's account suggests that in common with other Asian cultures early Nepalese royalty probably kept for themselves the privilege of wearing precious metals and stones. This use of dress and jewellery to mark social status continued into later centuries in Nepal and we know that during the Malla period (1200-1768) the untouchable caste were forbidden to wear gold, the law required them to wear iron and live outside settlements.[7]

With the exception of the Tibetan north, most of the jewellery forms of Nepal and especially those of the Kathmandu Valley reflect those of India. This is a legacy of two

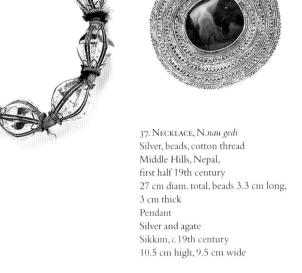

37. NECKLACE, N. *nau gedi*
Silver, beads, cotton thread
Middle Hills, Nepal,
first half 19th century
27 cm diam. total, beads 3.3 cm long,
3 cm thick
Pendant
Silver and agate
Sikkim, *c.*19th century
10.5 cm high, 9.5 cm wide

At the centre of the necklace is a large bell-shaped bead filled with pitch, which has red seeds pressed into it for decoration. The other barrel-shaped fluted beads are also made of thin silver over a pitch filling. These are worn mostly by western Tamang women of the Middle Hills. The pendant was worn by the indigenous Lepcha women of Sikkim. As the grains of silver decorating its surface between lines of pearled wire are so tiny, making soldering too messy, it is likely that true granulation has been used. In this technique, practised in the Himalayas only in eastern Nepal, adjoining Sikkim, the surfaces of two metals are fused by heat and a catalyst alone.
Acquired by the East India Company Museum in 1855. V&A: IS 03073
Bequest of Lord Curzon.
V&A: IM 179-1927

millennia of trade, the movement of peoples and strong dynastic contacts from the south. The early migrations of Hindu and Buddhist refugees and Indian rulers who seized power or maintained marriage contacts with their homeland all helped to spread Indian styles. Rulers such as Sithiti Malla (r.1382-95) from northern Bihar, who unified the Kathmandu Valley, would have brought their family jewellery and goldsmiths and the Indian jewellery, which royalty and

38. IMAGE ADORNED WITH JEWELLERY
Approximately 2m high
Patan, Kathmandu Valley, Nepal, 2000

A modern-crowned Buddha image with embossed and jewelled crown, dressed in robes and wearing separately made earrings, a *suta* necklace and the heavy silver chain called *sikha*. This contemporary image shows ancient traditions and skills being carried forward into the next century.

aristocrats must have continued to wear, would have been gradually adopted or incorporated by their host societies. In many cases the jewellery types brought to Nepal are still worn in India today. The *tilhari* wedding necklace and multiple round-hoop earrings worn in western Nepal are identical to those worn in Rajasthan while the torque necklaces of western India and the cuff bracelets of the western and eastern states mirror those worn by the Newars. The Indian prototypes of several key Newar forms – the wide gorget necklace or *suta*, the cuff bracelets and necklaces with jewels hanging from their lower edges or *tikma* – all appear in stylized form on sculptures made in north and east India between the ninth and twelfth centuries.[8] They are mirrored in Newar art from the same centuries onwards.[9] By the seventeenth century painting and metal sculpture, particularly of royal donor figures, begins to clearly reflect the wider variety of types worn today.[10] *Suta* and *tayo* necklaces, hair ornaments, round and stud earrings and cuff bracelets are all in evidence, and are mentioned in a list of jewellery worn by the queen of King Bupatindra Malla in the seventeenth century.[11] Today most are used only for the rituals that mark the major events in a person's life but it is this ceremonial jewellery that particularly sets Newar ornament apart from that of other Middle Hills peoples. Although some forms are related to other ethnic groups in Nepal, the large necklaces and elaborate head ornaments of the Newar are uniquely their own. The majority of jewellery types shown in this book are worn by women in life-cycle ceremonies and by humans portraying gods or goddesses in religious dances and processions while similar pieces are used to adorn the images of deities (plate 38).

At many of the major ceremonies of a woman's life, including a girl's initiation ceremony, or *ihi*, at marriage, or *ihi pa*, and in the three rites of entering old age, or *burka janko*, the same basic set of ceremonial ornaments are used. On these occasions the *sir bandi* or head ornament (plate 39), the *tikma* necklace (plates 39, 40), the *tayo* or *toh* necklaces (plates 106, 107), the cuff bracelets (plate 39) and the *jantar* or amulet container (plates, 35, 36, 111) are all often seen. Other distinctive gold repoussé head ornaments, worn on the top or back of the head at marriage or the old-age ceremonies, are called *lunya swan*.[12] The broad, crescent-moon-shaped necklace called *suta* or *konchi* (plate 113) is worn by boys and girls at their initiation rites, *bare chuyigu* and *ihi* respectively, and is a constant decoration around the necks of religious images (plate 38).

The lozenge-shaped *tayo* (plates 42, 106) is perhaps the most famous necklace of the Kathmandu Valley and is unique

to the Newars. The main pendant is gold or copper-gilt worn horizontally from multiple yarn threads or, on the more elaborate *tayo bizakani,* supported on each side by bands of cotton embellished by sewn on gold plaques. As a powerful sacred ornament, *tayo* are appropriate for the adornment of deities and may be seen being worn by incarnations of the living goddess Kumari when attending public religious events. More frequently they are glimpsed around the necks of metal statues, especially Buddhist images such as Dipankara, the

39. YOUNG GIRL AT AN *ihi* CEREMONY
Kathmandu Valley, 1980s

Between the ages of seven and twelve girls celebrate a mock marriage to a form of the god Vishnu, symbolized by a bel fruit. This ritual, one of the most venerated by Newars, means that throughout her life a girl is protected from becoming a widow, since she is married to an immortal. It also establishes her right to divorce and re-marriage. She is shown wearing auspicious red clothes associated with marriage, the *tikma* necklace (plate 40), cuff bracelets, and the *sir bandi* head ornament. The latter consists of three bands of cloth covered with gold-embossed plates and the central *bindia* or *tika* marriage token.
Photograph by Hannelore Gabriel

40. CEREMONIAL NECKLACE, *tikma*
Gold backed with pitch, silver, silk cord, turquoise, coral, rubies, sapphires
Kathmandu Valley, Nepal, *c.*19th century
24 cm maximum width, plaques 4.8 cm tall

The *tikma* necklace worn by Newar women at many life-cycle ceremonies including *ihi,* or a girl's initiation (plate 39), and marriage and also seen around the necks of those portraying female deities at dances (plate 107). Separate embossed-gold plaques filled with pitch are hinged at the back. Usually these are sewn onto red felt which is missing on this piece. Matching turquoises from two very different sources have been combined here to provide a striking contrast, the pale pieces are each carved with representations of the Hindu god Vishnu on Garuda, his vehicle.
V&A: IM 92–1911

Buddha of the past epoch.

More widely used than these are *jantar,* or square amulet boxes of gold, silver or copper, that encase protective objects such as written mantras or prayers. The wearing of *kalli* or anklets is now much more limited than in the past: married women no longer, as previously, wear them up until the birth of their first child and they are worn only at weddings and for protection by children. In the Hindu tradition gold, with its divine associations, cannot be worn below the waist except by royalty or deities so anklets are made of silver or iron. These are thought suitable for wearing close to the feet which are polluted by contact with the ground. Women's anklets, worn now only at weddings, are often solid, massive and heavy and have simple knob or lion-headed terminals. Anklets made of iron are thought to protect their wearer from ghosts and evil spirits and are still considered essential for children. Bracelets *sinkhwa lun churi* (plate 104) are similar in form to anklets and may be hollow or solid with decorative lion terminals. Wider cuff bracelets, or *baju,* are 4 to 17 centimetres wide and made of two hinged pieces of ridged metal, ideally of gold but owing to its scarcity and cost today increasingly made of silver (plate 39).

Although large pieces of ceremonial jewellery are still kept by wealthy families, there is less jewellery worn on a day-to-day basis than several decades ago. The plethora of large and heavy earrings and necklaces worn in the first half of the twentieth century is no longer seen. A reduction in the size of pieces and in the way they are worn has come about as a result of several combined factors. Modernization and changes in taste have coincided with a huge population increase which has set rising demand against the small trickle of precious metals entering the country. As the traditional barter economy has given way to a cash one, when money for necessities is scarce old jewellery is often sold. An increasing tourist demand has led to the export of old pieces and a still further drain on gold supplies. There are also increasing concerns about the security risk involved in wearing large gold pieces which are now seldom seen on the streets. Women, perhaps conditioned by western norms, are now also more conscious of the distortions of the ears and nose that are caused by wearing heavy jewellery and, even in the country, wearing large quantities of silver ornaments is going out of fashion. Today small earrings, stud nose rings, a gold chain necklace and a simple pendant are often the only jewellery worn by a woman on a daily basis. Men never traditionally wore much jewellery; today some may wear a gold chain and a gold ring with an inset coral bead.[13]

## Craftsmen, Materials and Techniques

Chinese diplomatic missions who visited Nepal in 647 and 657 CE were impressed by the lavish use of pearls and precious stones decorating religious images in the capital and by the jewels worn by the king himself.[14] These were set with pearls, mother-of-pearl, coral, amber and jade. The Kathmandu Valley lies on a main trade route from India to Tibet and it is likely that from an early period it shared many of the same sources of imported gemstones as its larger neighbour to the north. We know that in the eighteenth and nineteenth centuries Hindu trading pilgrims brought south Indian pearls and other precious stones into Nepal and almost certainly the same seaborne imports to India supplied both Nepal and Tibet. A list of Indian exports to Nepal in 1830–1 shows that although a large percentage of the Mediterranean coral beads, Iranian turquoise and Baltic red and yellow amber were being traded on to Tibet, there was nevertheless a healthy demand for them in Nepal itself. This came not only from the Tibeto-Nepalese of the Himalayan borderlands but also from the peoples of the Middle Hills, both Indo-Nepalese and Tibeto-Burman. A difference in Tibetan and Nepalese taste is reflected in the same list of nineteenth-century exports which records that 100,000 Nepalese rupees worth of diamonds, emeralds, rubies and sapphires were consumed in Nepal in 1830 while none found their way to Tibet.[15]

In terms of human jewellery Newar taste was actually generally averse to large gem-set surfaces preferring the beauty of beaten and worked gold and silver. However, stones were used in the valley towns from medieval times onwards to enrich the surfaces of metal images and to carpet with precious and semi-precious stones the ceremonial jewellery of images and a wide variety of other objects. Together these factors, including the increasingly Indianized taste of the Rana aristocracy from the mid-nineteenth to the mid-twentieth century, help explain the large-scale importation of gems. Nepal does have deposits of ruby, garnet,[16] tourmaline and moonstone, and beryl and tourmaline have been mined at Chainpur in eastern Nepal for several decades. Rock crystal is mentioned by the Chinese envoy to Nepal in the seventh century as one of the stones used by the Nepalese king to adorn himself. There was evidently a large production of religious icons, stupas and *shri yantras* or mandala designs carved in clear quartz in the nineteenth century that suggests a local supply. Today, coral comes from Taiwan and many other stones, including imported Iranian turquoise, from Jaipur in Rajasthan.

Gold prized for its purity and beauty in the Hindu world,
was the most preferred and widely used metal by the Newars.
Nepal has always relied on gold-rich Tibet for its supplies as it
contains only minor alluvial deposits in the Kali Gandhaki and
the Kathmandu Valley rivers. Today these are panned secretly
by boatmen and fishermen as extraction is illegal. The precious
metal is also recovered from the earth, under the eaves of
temples with gilded roofs and from the dust of goldsmiths'
workshop floors. A special group of Shakyas called Dhoosas
buy the earth and recover gold, silver and copper by a
series of washing, separating and melting processes.[17]
Today gold is also imported from India but until recently
any importation was illegal. Like gold, silver was mostly
imported from Tibet in the past. Nepal's second largest
source was the Indian silver rupee.[18] Up until the late
nineteenth century Nepal was rich in copper and
exported the metal to Tibet, but throughout the twentieth
century copper was mainly imported from India.[19] Its use
in jewellery making has always been very limited and mainly
confined to act as a base for gilding to cut down on the cost
of large ceremonial gold jewellery.

Newar goldsmiths in the Kathmandu Valley are almost all
of the highest or Banra caste, the descendants of Indian

42. WOMAN'S NECK ORNAMENT, *tayo bizakani*
Brass and turquoise
Made by Astaman Sakya, 2000
Lozenge pendant10 cm long

A newly made piece prior to fire
gilding, with stones temporarily laid
into settings. This is a version of the
more elaborate form of *tayo* (plate 107)
the *tayo bizakani* which always features
the nine-(or up to thirteen-) headed
protective cobra raised above a jewel
setting. A meshed brass necklace replaces
the more usual cloth supports covered
with embossed gold or gilded plaques.
This was made for a Newar family using
gilded rather than pure gold ornaments
as is increasingly common today.

Buddhist monks. The majority are Shakyas with smaller
numbers of the priestly Vajracharyas or 'vajra masters'. Most
Banras live and work in Patan with smaller groups in
Kathmandu and Bhaktapur. Outside of the valley they
monopolize the making and selling of metalwares throughout
the towns of the Middle Hills. But in the valley towns they
continue to live in the *baha* or *bahals*, complexes of dwellings
built around a temple and courtyard that were the former
Buddhist monasteries. Shakya goldsmiths generally work in
the open-fronted ground floors of their own homes or in the
adjoining courtyards. Most work is commissioned by
individual shopkeepers, or today by exporters. In many cases
the same craftsmen make jewellery for both Hindu and
Buddhist Nepalese patrons and for Tibetan Buddhist refugees.

The tools, general working methods and layout of a Newar
gold or silversmith's workshop is similar to that of a Tibetan
metalworker and many processes are also closely paralleled.
Gold is either bought from the goldsmith or brought in by the
client as broken or damaged scrap jewellery to be recycled.
Instead of a cash payment, it is common for craftsmen to keep
a small percentage of the precious metal as raw material. The
same pitch (N. *jhau*) required for repoussé work (*tappal* or
*tronjah*) is used to fill beads and other pieces covered with thin
gold to make the metal go further.[20] In order to minimize the
loss of gold, filing and sawing is kept to an absolute minimum
and when necessary carried out over a piece of paper or other
container so that filings can be saved for re-melting. With care
many traditional shapes such as *dhungri* earrings (plate 105) can
be cut from the sheet with shears and without the need for
filing. As in Tibet gold with a rich reddish glow is valued and
this is imparted to a finished gold piece by brushing it in a
solution of red ochre. After the piece has dried, it is heated
gently and brushed clean again in water to give the gold the
required red tinge.[21]

The *jarao* or stone-inlay technique, so well represented
here, involves the use of gold, silver or brass wire which is
beaten into thin strips. These are then cut into tiny circles that
form the different-shaped cloisons according to the part of the
design being formed: for example, the tail feathers of the
peacock in plate 110 required long, slender compartments,
while its head needed a tear shape. Spirals, or shikon, U shapes,
or *palicha*, and circles, or *fakon*, are the most common shapes.
The piece to be decorated then has solder and borax flux
applied to the cloisons either in powder, solution or solid form,
after which it is heated to fuse the whole wire tracery together.
When cool, stones of the right shape are selected or cut to fill

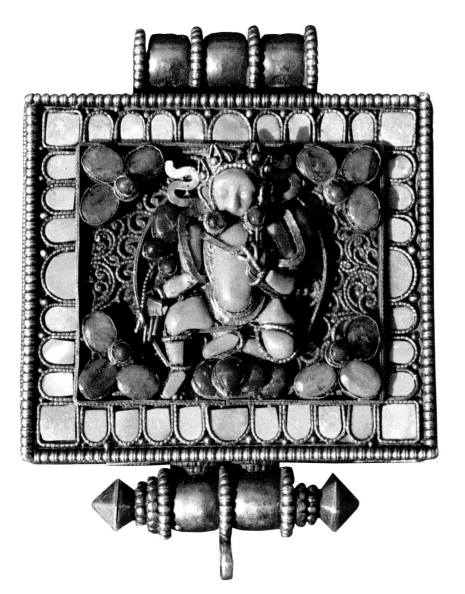

43. AMULET BOX, *ga'u*
Copper-gilt,
turquoise, coral
Patan, Kathmandu
Valley, 2000
7 cm long, 5 cm wide

A modern version of
a Tibetan *ga'u* nears
completion. This one
is being made for the
western market by a
present-day Newar
stone carver although
the combination of
filigree and stones set
into metal cloisons is
an ancient Newari
one. The time-
consuming nature
of shaping and
polishing tiny stones
is illustrated by the
craftsman's comment
that the face of the
seated Bodhisattva had
taken him three days
alone.

the metal bezels and are set into *jhau* mastic.[22]

In older examples of *jarao* individual stones that depict faces or other important parts of the figure are often finely carved. The skill of Newar stone carvers was praised by western visitors to Lhasa during the nineteenth century and is apparent on many of the pieces in this book. Although this tradition was reported to be dying in Nepal during the early 1980s[23], an increase in demand from dealers ordering for the export market in Hong Kong, Taiwan and the West has led to something of a revival. Some of the wealthier cutters use machine-driven, carbon-steel Indian saws and corundum disks to cut and shape stones. Although many have the metalworking skills to enable them to make finished jewellery, there are also those who specialize only in fine stone carving (plate 43), depicting Hindu and Buddhist deities, flowers and animals. Iron tools are used with abrasive powders to carve coral, turquoise, bone, ivory, tourmaline and jade. Stones are stuck onto the end of sticks with *jhau* mastic which allow them to be fixed into a vice or clamp for carving. The present generation of carvers remember their fathers using hand-held, bamboo bow drills. But to pierce stones today they use a hand-operated drill similar to the old-fashioned, European wood drills.

# Lhasa

**44. OFFICIAL'S NEW YEAR EAR ORNAMENTS**
Part of the ornaments of the ancient kings, *ringyen*
Silver-gilt, turquoise, lapis lazuli, coral, rubies, white sapphire, rock crystal, carnelian
Lhasa, *c.* 18th or 19th century
9.5 cm high, bottom circle 6.5 cm diam.

Two ceremonial earrings of the type worn by noblemen since the 17th century at the New Year ceremonies in Lhasa. At this time officials dressed in what were believed to be the ornaments of the early kings of Tibet (7th to 9th centuries) (see page 22). These large earrings were far too heavy to be worn conventionally and were tied across the head or draped around the neck. The pale turquoises covering IM 83–1911 evoke the concentric open petals of a lotus while both pieces bear the protective monster mask often found on these ornaments. The ubiquity of similarly modelled masks on ceremonial Newar jewellery suggests that Newars were responsible for these pieces. Purchased from Imre Schwaiger. V&A: IM 83–1911, IM 88–1911

**45. CEREMONIAL NEW YEAR EAR ORNAMENTS**

Formerly owned by Wangchen Gelek Surkhang

Gold, turquoise, coral, agate, silk thread

Lhasa, 18th century or later

Round earring: 11.5 cm long, piece with attached tassels: 16 cm long.

The personal ceremonial earrings of a junior official who later became one of the four most important cabinet ministers or *Shapés* of the inner cabinet. The round turquoise-covered ear ornament was worn at the right shoulder, the other piece with the coral and turquoise beads and tassels at the left shoulder. Plate 46 shows Surkhang wearing what appear to be these very ornaments during New Year 1937.

Ashmolean Museum, Oxford

48. OFFICIAL'S HAIR AMULET BOX,
*taghab*
Silver-gilt and turquoise
Lhasa, c.first half of the 19th
century (right)
5.3 cm long, 3.6 cm wide

Government officials of the
Fourth Rank and above in the
Lhasa government wore this
distinctive type of small oval *ga'u*
in their braided hair (plate 47)
as a symbol of rank. They were
tied, edge on, with the
turquoise-covered front side
outwards, between the two
plaited hair knots on top of the
head. There is a Sherpa legend
that the practice originated with
the kings of ancient Tibet.[12]
Most *ta ghab* are made of gold
but the same type was also made
in brass and used to decorate the
queues of the servants of
officials and noblemen.
Acquired by the East India
Company Museum in 1855.
V&A: 03051

46. WANGCHEN GELEK SURKHANG
WEARING THE ORNAMENTS OF THE
ANCIENT KINGS, *ringyen*
Lhasa, 1937

A young official during the New
Year ceremonies wearing the
*gyaluche* or 'garments of royalty',
believed to be the dress of the
early Tibetan kings, which
included a short brocade jacket,
coloured scarf and white papier-
mâché hat imitating a turban.[10]
The round ceremonial earrings,
worn together with the usual
long official's earring, are
probably the set held today in the
Ashmolean Museum, Oxford
(plate 45) At other times this very
valuable jewellery and costume
was kept in the treasury of the
Potala Palace and a member of
the cabinet, or *Kashag*, checked
its issue and return.
Photograph by Frederick
Spencer Chapman. Pitt Rivers
Museum, University of Oxford

47. LHASA OFFICIAL WEARING *ga'u,*
*tagab* OR *takor,* AND EARRING, *sochi*
Photograph 1936

Only officials of the fourth rank
and upwards were allowed to tie
their hair up in two braided
knots, or *pachok,* which were
interwoven with red ribbon.
Oval amulets were tied onto the
front of these knots with the
turquoise – covered side facing
outwards.[11] The idea behind the
placing of amulets in this position
was that the written prayers
contained within them would
help both to protect the wearer
and to sanctify his actions. The
servants of officials often wore
similar *ga'us* made of a cheaper
material attached to their queues.
Officials of all ranks wore the
long thin earrings.
Photograph by Frederick
Spencer Chapman. Pitt Rivers
Museum, University of Oxford

49. OFFICIAL'S EARRING, *sochi*
Gold, pearl, turquoise and glass
Lhasa, 19th century (far right)
16.8 cm long, 4.5 cm wide

All lay officials wore the thin,
pencil-shaped, gold and
turquoise earring with a pearl at
its centre and a glass turquoise-
coloured drop, there being a law
forbidding the use of actual
turquoise for this. These were
worn in the left ear, the gold
hoop fitting through the pierced
ear while a silk cord fitting over
the ear helped to take some of
the weight. The same long
pencil-shaped earring was also a
symbol of government office
amongst officials in the
principality of Sakya in southern
Tibet.[13] Postmen, undertakers
and the servants of officials
could also wear brass versions of
this type of earring.

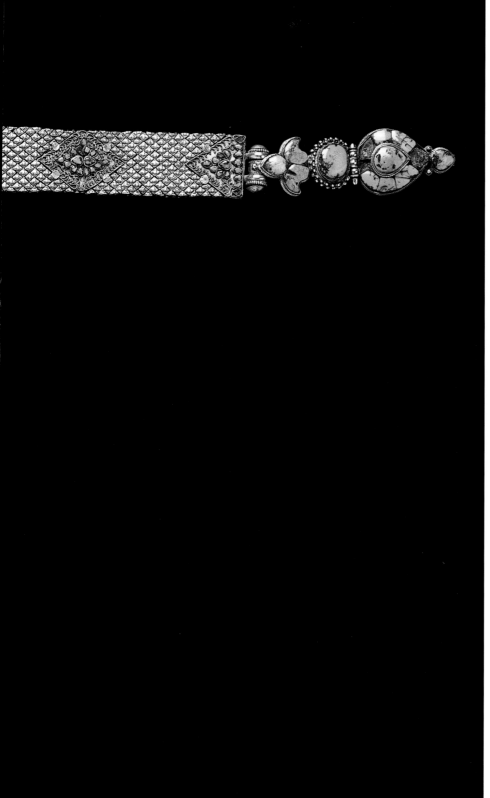

50. WOMAN'S WAIST
ORNAMENT, *gyenzen*
Silver and gilt copper,
turquoise
Central Tibet, *c.*19th or
early 20th century
71 cm max. length, central
hanger 30 cm long,
3 cm wide

One of the most eye-
catching ornaments worn at
waist level by noble women
in Lhasa was this T-shaped,
flexible belt composed of
separately cast silver links
and set with plaques
covered with turquoises.
On important occasions
long strings of turquoise,
coral and pearl beads were
attached from the wheel-
like end of the central strap
which hung down at the
front (plate 53). These
looped on one side, or on
both, almost down to the
ankles and back up to hook
into the main garment
under the shoulder. This
piece cleverly and unusually
incorporates Lhasa women's
earrings to form decorative
terminals at each end.
Bequest of Lord Curzon.
V&A: IM 303 – 1927

51. WOMAN'S 'EIGHT-
CORNERED' AMULET BOX,
*ga'u zurgyad*
Copper-gilt, turquoise and
imitation precious stones
Made by Chozai, Gangtok,
1960–80
8 cm square

*Ga'u*s of this Maltese Cross,
or eight-armed star shape,
became fashionable in
Lhasa during the 1940s and
1950s and are made today
for members of the Tibetan
community in exile. The
ex-Lhasa jeweller Chozai
who lives in Gangtok,
Sikkim, made this example.
Women often placed a
prize *ga'u* at the centre of a
necklace of turquoise, coral
and *dzi* beads. More *ga'u*s
were worn on important
occasions to increase the
dressy effect of a woman's
costume.

52. Woman's necklace and amulet box, *ga'u thub zhi*
Gold, silver, *dzi*, turquoise, zircon (?), rubies, coral
Box 11 cm square

The classic Lhasa women's *ga'u*[14] whose form of two intersecting squares symbolizes two crossed *dorjes*, the S.*visvavajra*, symbol of the ultimate stability of Buddhahood. The symmetrical arrangement of shaped and polished turquoises and precious stones is typical. Fashionable in Lhasa from at least the middle of the 19th century, this type of *ga'u* grew increasingly elaborate and larger in size with time, reaching its apogee in the 1940s (plate 51).
Gift of Mrs Bailey. National Museums Liverpool

53. TWO LHASA
NOBLEWOMEN
Photograph, 1921

These two aristocratic
young women are probably
wearing almost their full set
of jewellery, only worn on
the most formal of
occasions.[15] In addition to
the headdress, amulet box
and large earrings there is
the long *kyetreng* necklace
made up of jades, corals and
turquoises reaching to the
waist. It is held in the
correct position by being
hooked up to another
ornament, the *yarthen*, its
many strings of seed pearls
held parallel by turquoise-
set gold plaques. Other
body-length necklaces of
semi-precious stones are
attached to the bottom arm
of the waist ornament or
*gyenzen*. The full set of
ornaments worn by a
noblewoman could be
extremely valuable, and
when walking through
busy city streets, required
an accompanying servant
to prevent theft.[16]
Pitt Rivers Museum,
University of Oxford

54. WOMAN'S NECKLACE OF
FAKE *dzi* BEADS AND AMULET
BOX, *ga'u thub zhi*
Silver, pearls, turquoise,
and glass
Lhasa, *c.*20th century
*Ga'u:* 10 cm long, 10 cm
wide, 2.6 cm deep
Necklace: 36 cm long

From the 1930s onwards in
Lhasa pillow-shaped *ga'us*
such as this, a variant of the
older square shape, became
popular. Silver pearled wire,
pearls, turquoise and
imitation corals cover a
silver-gilt base. The
necklace is of imitation
glass *dzi* beads.
Pitt Rivers Museum,
University of Oxford

55. Wife of the Gyantse
Dzongpon (District
Governor)
1936

The Lhasa-style earrings
and *patruk* headdress are
being worn with an amulet
box and hanging ornament.
Corals and turquoises were
drilled and stitched onto
the rolled cotton or wood
or leather armatures, the
pearls attached in strings
along the three sides. Before
the age of puberty, girls
wore their hair in a single
plait to which stones were
attached. The same stones,
together with new pieces,
were fixed to the *patruk* a
girl was given to symbolize
her coming of responsible
age – sometime between
the years of 15 and 20. The
donning of the *patruk*
occurred at the *patruk*
ceremony which formally
marked this rite of passage.
Photograph by Frederick
Spencer Chapman. Pitt
Rivers Museum, University
of Oxford

56. Pair of women's
earrings, *akor*
Silver and turquoise
Lhasa, 19th century
12 cm long, 4 cm wide

Lhasa woman wore this
type of ear ornament with
ends in the form of stylized
lotus buds. Called *akor* they
hung at either side of the
face hiding both ears and
facing forwards to show
their inset stones. Due to
their considerable weight,
they were either attached
with small hooks to the
headdress or hung over the
head. This type is found as a
decoration on the sides of
the tombs of the 11th
(1838–56), 12th (1856–75)
and 13th (1876–1933)
Dalai Lamas in the Potala
Palace.
Bought from Annie Taylor.
National Museums of
Scotland

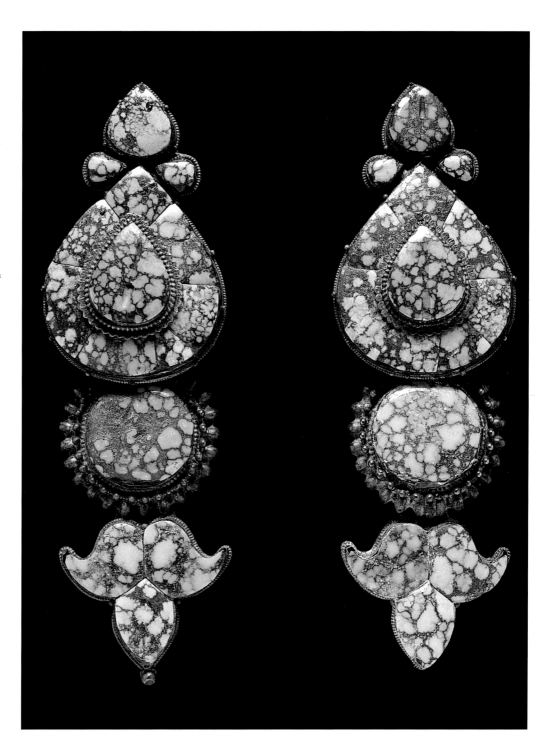

57. PAIR OF WOMEN'S
EARRINGS, *along*
Silver, turquoise and coral
Lhasa, 19th century
12 cm long, 4 cm wide,

A popular earring type
during the 19th and 20th
centuries worn by women
in both central Tibet and
the Chamdo area of eastern
Tibet.
Bought from Annie Taylor.
National Museums of
Scotland

58. WOMAN'S HEADDRESS,
*patruk*
Coral, turquoise
and seed pearls
Lhasa, 20th century
36.5 cm long, 33 cm wide,
3 cm deep

The horned *patruk*
headdress was a Lhasa style,
worn with the two points at
each side of the head and
tied on with the cords
visible here (plate 55).
Fashion also affected
headdresses and before
about 1930 these were
much flatter in form.
This is the richest seed-
pearl-covered type of *patruk*
*(mutik patruk)*, which was
for special occasions while
there was a coral and
turquoise *patruk* for
everyday wear. Although
mainly worn by the
noblewomen of Lhasa, the
wives of wealthy traders
also adorned themselves
with the *mutik patruk* when
funds permitted.
Cambridge Museum of
Archaeology and
Anthropology

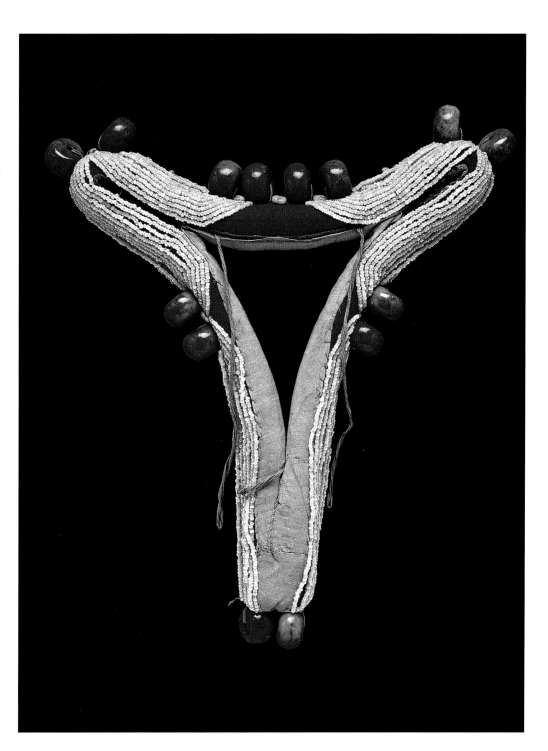

59. BACKVIEW OF LHASA
WOMAN, *c.*1930–49

A rarely seen view that
shows how the triangular
Lhasa headdress or *patruk*
was worn and reveals the
waist ornament of multiple
silver chains hanging at the
back. A wig of false hair was
attached to each of the
*patruk's* front corners and
fell loose to the shoulders.
From there it was gathered
in several braids bound with
coloured string and then
descended at each side
nearly to the knees. It was
very important for women
to have corals and
turquoises matching in
colour and size on their
*patruks* and stones might be
taken from older family
headdresses and necklaces
or bought over a number of
years.[17]
© The British Museum

60. WAIST ORNAMENT
Silver, silver-gilt, turquoise,
rubies, sapphires, beryl
Probably Lhasa,
early 20th century
48 cm maximum length,
22 cm length of drop

This was one of the most
spectacular but seldom
worn of the sixteen types
of Lhasa women's
ornaments.[18] The way this
was worn hanging at the
back of the waist is revealed
by a recently discovered
photograph (plate 59).
The piece probably evolved
from the former custom of
hanging a purse and needle
case at each side at the back
of the body as is still
sometimes done in eastern
Tibet. At the centre of the
oval plaque is the motif of
the legendary 'Wish-
Fulfilling Jewel', or *yid zhin
norbu,* here shown by a
setting of three turquoises
and a green beryl. Each of
the multiple chain links are
in the form of miniature
*dorjes* or 'diamond sceptres'.
Purchased from Imre
Schwaiger. V&A: IM
385–1914

**61. MAN AND WOMAN'S AMULET BOX,** *ga'u*
Copper and copper gilt turquoise and 8 rubies
Probably central or southern Tibet, *c.*19th century
Larger 24 cm high, 20 cm wide, 6 cm deep
Smaller 9.5 cm high, 9.5 cm wide, 1.5 cm deep

Although both these amulet boxes are standard Tibetan forms, their workmanship clearly reveals that they were made by Nepalese craftsmen, perhaps working for Tibetan patrons while resident in a Tibetan town. Not only is the style of the scrollwork and the 'Eight Auspicious Emblems' around the central figure of the Bodhisattva Avalokitesvara markedly Nepalese, but the surrounding door-pillars and imitation brickwork actually look like temple architecture of the Kathmandu Valley. The woman's square Lhasa-style *ga'u* is set with a coral carved with an eight-armed Tantric figure, a form of decoration typically found on Newar jewellery. Purchased from Imre Schwaiger. Large *ga'u,* V&A: IM 26–1955; small *ga'u,* V&A: IM 171–1910

**62. MAN'S AMULET BOX,** *ga'u dawang*
Silver and silver-gilt, copper, painted clay
Lhasa, *c.*late 19th or early 20th century
24 cm high, 18 cm wide, 8.5 cm deep

A large travelling *ga'u* exquisitely embossed with flowering tendrils and the type of sprig leaves favoured by Lhasa goldsmiths. Within the scrollwork are the 'Eight Auspicious Emblems' of Buddhism and below the central window, as an offering to the deities within, the 'Five Sense Symbols', *dod yon nya,* comprising sight (mirror), hearing (lute), smell (incense), taste (food) and touch (cloth). At the bottom is the protective monster mask and mountain and sea design and at the top the 'Wish-Fulfilling Jewel'. This box encloses a stamped and gold-painted clay relief of the group of the twenty-one Taras, female goddesses who offer protection from a range of misfortune.
Bequest of Lord Curzon.
V&A: IM 133–1927

# Central and Southern Tibet

63. WOMAN'S HEADDRESS,
*pagor*
Turquoise, coral, white glass,
brass, cane and felt, human
hair
Southern Tibet,
*c.*19th century
33 cm high, 50 cm wide

The headdress of a woman
from southern Tibet, Tsang.
The cane structure is covered
in red felt with strands of
'pearls' simulated with white
glass beads. False plaits of
human hair are attached at
each side. The extraordinary
horn-shaped women's
headdresses of central and
southern Tibet may have pre-
Buddhist origins and remind
one of the silver-encased hair
constructions of the Kalkha
Mongols shaped like the
horns of the wild sheep, *Ovis
ammon,* which one scholar
traces back to the Sino-
Siberian Iron Age.[19] A
common ancient ancestry for
Tibetan and Mongolian
headdresses is far from
improbable, though the 600-
year-long history of
Mongolian intervention in
Tibetan political and religious
affairs spanning the 13th to
the 18th centuries make a
later borrowing from
Mongolia also quite possible.
This historical connection
was certainly celebrated by
the use of specially rich
Mongolian style costumes
worn by the *Yasos,* officials in
charge of the New Year
celebrations in Lhasa.
National Museums of
Scotland

64. WOMAN FROM SOUTHERN
TIBET, 1920–21

A lady from southern Tibet
wearing the most elaborate
and expensive type of
headdress, or *pagor*, from
that region. Only on the
richest was the arched area
completely filled, as here,
with multiple strings of
freshwater pearls. The
higher the headdress the
more fashionable it was
considered, although even
moderate *pagor* were
unwieldy and liable to be
blown awry in high winds.
They required stabilizing
with hooks and cords at the
back. Hair was braided into
many tiny plaits and hung
down from where it was
fixed at each side of the
arch.
Photograph by W. P.
Rosemeyer. Pitt Rivers
Museum, University of
Oxford

65. PAIR OF WOMEN'S
EARRINGS, *along*
Silver and turquoise
Lhasa, *c.*late 19th century
4 cm in diameter

This is one of the most
popular types of earring
worn throughout Tibet in
pairs by women and singly
by men. The hoops are
made from pearled wire, the
bezels decorated with
separately added silver
granulation. As they were
heavy to wear, the weight
was taken by a chain or
thread hooking them up
into the hair or even over
the head. Each has a small
ring under the bezel by
which the chain was
attached.
Acquired during the 1904
British expedition to Lhasa.
V&A: IM 12&a1911

66. MEN'S EARRINGS
Silver and turquoise
Guru, central Tibet, early
20th century
upper: shank 5.3 cm long,
bezel 3.6 cm long
lower: shank 4.2 cm long,
bezel 4.1 cm long

Stylish variants of the
normal man's earring with
lotus-shaped, turquoise-
covered plaques. They are
not a pair but part of a
larger group given by
Sargent Heaney, a member
of the British military
expedition to Lhasa in
1904. This fact, together
with the place of
acquisition, the site of a
battle, suggests they were
collected from the
battlefield by him during
the British advance on
Lhasa.
National Museums
Liverpool

67. NOMAD MAN WEARING
HOOP EARRING, *along*
Ladakh, *c.*late 20th century

The most popular men's
earring in Tibet and
Ladakh, a circle of pearled
wire set with a single
turquoise facing outward.
This man is probably saying
prayers as he is fingering the
rosary around his neck
while the photograph is
being taken.
© Diane Barker/Tibet
Images

68. WOMAN'S AMULET BOX,
*ga'u*
Silver, copper, coral and
turquoise
Tibet, *c.*early 20th century
10 cm long, 8 cm wide, 3
cm deep

The front of this amulet
box is covered in separately
embossed or stamped
filigree sprigs, flower and
petal elements. Though
retaining their functions as
containers for relics,
women's *ga'u*s always have a
role as pieces of jewellery
and tend to be more
decorative than the
equivalent men's boxes.
Bequest of Lord Curzon,
acquired in Sikkim. V&A:
IM 177–1927

69. AMULET BOX, *ga'u*
Copper, brass and coral
Tibet, *c.*19th or 20th
century
9 cm long, 11.5 cm wide,
3.5 cm deep

Beaded, openwork brass
scrolls radiate from a central
coral, overlaid against a
copper background. The
*ga'u* contains a block-
printed charm featuring the
magical numbers of the
nine planets and the eight
trigrams derived from the *I
Ching* which together guard
against adverse planetary
influences.
V&A: IS 14&a1965

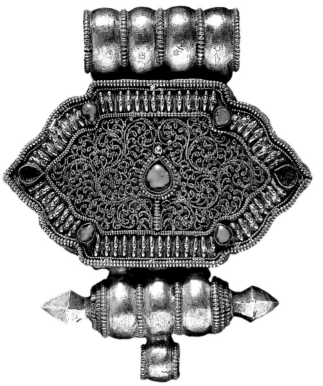

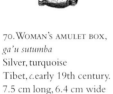

70. WOMAN'S AMULET BOX,
*ga'u sutumba*
Silver, turquoise
Tibet, *c.*early 19th century.
7.5 cm long, 6.4 cm wide

This type of rectangular
*ga'u* called *sutumba* or
*surdewa* was very popular in
the border areas of west and
south Tibet, and in the
Indian Himalayan districts
of Spiti and Lahul. The
central field of filigree wire
surrounding a stylized lotus
bud with a central turquoise
is typical of the decoration
found on this type of
amulet box. On all *ga'u*s the
stylized *dorje* ornament
always hangs at the bottom
when worn.
Obtained in Kathmandu in
1855. V&A: 13054

71. WOMAN'S AMULET BOX,
*ga'u kerima*
Silver
Probably Sikkim, first half
of 19th century
8.5 cm long, 6 cm wide

Although worn in all areas,
the oval-shaped silver *ga'u*
called a *kerima* (*khedi* in
Lhasa) was particularly
favoured by women in the
southern border areas of
Tibet, in Sikkim and
Bhutan. The name is
derived from *khal* meaning

kidney, a reflection of its
shape. Many women's *ga'u*s
including this one have a
loop at the bottom from
which hung suspended
ornaments or decorative
chains that hooked up to
shoulder level. A plainer
version of this pleasing *ga'u*
form was worn by nuns
throughout Tibet.
Acquired in Sikkim by the
East India Company
Museum in 1855. V&A:
03065 IS

# Eastern Tibet

72. AMULET CASE, *ga'u*
Copper and brass
Chamdo, eastern Tibet,
*c.*early 20th century
11.5 cm long, 15 cm wide,

This beautiful container
displays the typical Tibetan
decorative effect where one
metal is overlaid on
another, here brass against
copper. The central symbol
is the *dorje* representing
enlightenment with an
auspicious conch below it.
Around each edge is a
protective mantra in the
archaic Lantsa script.
V&A: IM 77–1929

73. TINDER POUCHES, *mechag*
Steel, gold, brass and leather
Eastern Tibet,
*c.*19th century
left, 18.5 cm long,
8.3 cm wide
right, 12 cm long,
6 cm wide

Until the mid-20th century tinder pouches were widely used in Tibet where they were carried hung from the belt. Steel ridges at the bottom of the pouches enabled a spark to be struck using the flint and dry tinder was carried within. The piece on the right is enlivened with auspicious dragons chasing a jewel, skilfully executed in inlaid gold on iron, a technique for which the craftsmen of eastern Tibet were famous. The swastika is an ancient Indian auspicious emblem also used in Tibet. The other pouch is decorated with two facing deer in brass which look back to the prehistoric animal style of the Sino-Siberian steppes.
Bequest of Adelaine Gourlay. V&A: IS 26–1965, IS 28–1965

74. BELT ORNAMENTS, *lochab*
Silver, silver-gilt, coral and leather
Eastern Tibet, *c.*19th century
31.5 cm long, 12 cm maximum width

A pair of woman's belt ornaments from eastern Tibet which continue to be worn in the area especially at festival times (plate 76). They are suspended, one at each side of the body, from a belt and are decorated with tassels or chains that hook up to a central purse or other ornament. The embossed silverwork contains representations of jewels, evoking wealth, and protective monster masks. These typically eastern-Tibetan objects were acquired at Tashilunpo monastery in southern Tibet, making it likely that they were former donations of visiting pilgrims from the east of the country. Obtained on the 1904 British Expedition to Tibet.
V&A: 411&a–1906

75. Belt ornament, *lochab*, and tinder pouch, *mechag*
Silver, steel, coral, turquoise
Eastern Tibet, *c.*early 20th century
Belt hanger: 22.5 cm long
Tinder pouch: 12.7 cm long

A woman's belt hanger decorated with scrollwork surrounding a central turquoise. The jaws of a monster mask at the bottom of the embossed silver plaque hold a silver-looped ornament from which hangs a tinder pouch. *Mechag* from Kham are amongst the most beautifully decorated in Tibet, the settings of large coral beads in silver petal ornaments is typical of centres such as Derge.
© Copyright The British Museum

76. Woman of the Gaba area, Eastern Tibet, Yushu, 2003

A woman at festival time wearing two pairs of belt hangers at each side, front and back, over her otter skin dress, or *chupa*. The 'Two Fish' emblem with chains and miniature fish ornaments suspended from the front belt hanger is typically eastern Tibetan. An ornamental silver chain hung with bells links the back hangers to a purse at the centre of her waist. She also wears several coral necklaces and a single amber and coral head ornament.

77. TEENAGE BOY OF EASTERN TIBET, YUSHU, 2003

Though the rest of this ensemble is mostly seen only at festivals, the coiled queue wrapped with red braid and threaded with rings is commonly worn by men throughout the area. The queue rings worn here are of ivory, silver and coral. The boy also wears *dzi* and coral necklaces and a bone or ivory rosary, a ring on every finger and another rosary wrapped around his right wrist. Machismo demands the sword stuck through the waistband, his right hand rests on its hilt. A purse with hanging chains and stylized fish hangs at waist level and is linked to other ornaments at his back.

78. MAN'S QUEUE RING, *gyu ya*
Silver, dyed coral
Chamdo, eastern Tibet, 2003
7 cm high, 5 cm wide

This type of ring is threaded into the queues of men as decoration in eastern Tibet, often in groups of two or three. The queue is worn coiled around the head and threaded with red braid to enlarge it (plate 77) or a separate, false, queue-shaped hairpiece may be worn. The ring was made by a craftsman from Yunnan living in Chamdo who, like many other Yunnanese silversmiths, makes traditional jewellery for Tibetan patrons.
V&A: IS 17–2003

80. WOMAN'S HEAD
ORNAMENT, *melong pongu* OR
*metok*
Copper-gilt, silver-gilt,
dyed turquoise matrix
Derge, eastern Tibet, 2003
8.5 cm diam., 5.5 cm high

The largest version of the
*metok* or 'flower' ornament,
usually worn singly on the
front of the head by women
in the Derge and Chamdo
areas of eastern Tibet (plate
79). At festival times a pair
may be worn, one at the
front and one at the back of
the head joined by a line of
turquoises and corals
attached to the hair. The
dish-shaped plaque is
enriched with circles of
pearled and plaited silver
wire. Made by a Chinese
craftsman from Yunnan
living and working in
Derge town.
V&A: IS 18–1999

79. WOMAN WEARING HEAD
ORNAMENT, *melong pongu* OR
*metok*
Copper-gilt, silver-gilt,
dyed turquoise matrix
Derge, eastern Tibet, 2003

This woman wears the
typical head ornaments of
the Derge and Chamdo
region in eastern Tibet.
The metal is copper-gilt
decorated with pearled wire
and a central turquoise,
favoured in Derge. Coral is
more popular in Chamdo.

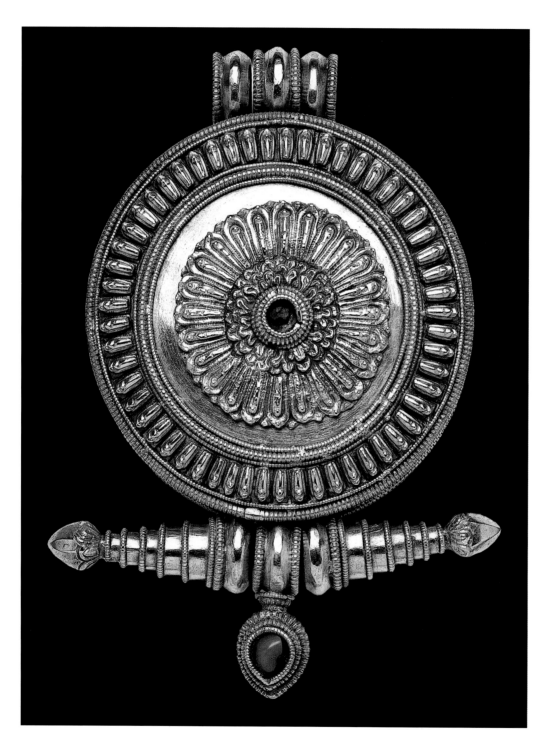

81. AMULET BOX, *ga'u*
Silver and coral
North-east Tibet, *c.*first half
of the 19th century
17.5 cm maximum length,
pendant 10.8 cm diam

A round *ga'u* of the type
worn by both nomad men
and women in north-
eastern Tibet called simply
*go go* or *gor-mo*, meaning
'round'. Its surface is
covered with concentric
silver-embossed elements
representing the petals of an
open lotus, symbol of
purity and spiritual power.
V&A: 02085

82. MAN'S EARRING, *along*
Silver, coral and turquoise
Eastern Tibet, *c.*early 19th
century
8 cm long (left)

MAN'S EARRING, *along*
Silver and turquoise
Tibet, *c.*late 19th century
2.5 cm diam. (centre)

WOMAN'S EARRING, *chusin
kamo*
Silver and coral
Batang area, eastern Tibet,
*c.*early 20th century
2.25 cm long (right)

The shaped turquoise on
the bottom ring is set into a
bezel decorated with
granulation. Throughout
Tibet and Ladakh men who
were not of noble status,
and therefore not allowed
to wear the pencil-shaped
earring, wore instead a
round, pearled wire hoop in
their left ear.
Above are two
characteristically eastern
Tibetan earrings, to the
right a style worn by the
women in the border area
of Batang in eastern Tibet.
Two stylised facing *chusin* or
sea monsters, which give
their name to this earring,
hold a coral bead between
them. On the left a man's
earring of the type worn in
eastern Tibet.
Man's earring (straight),
collected by Captain
Hamilton.
© Copyright The British
Museum

83. YOUNG WOMAN OF GABA,
eastern Tibet, Yushu, 2003

This shows another way of
adorning the head in
eastern Tibet using a single,
large ball of amber and a
smaller ball of coral linked
by strings of small turquoise
beads to the earrings. These
are a modern version of
traditional earrings worn in
the area, probably made by
Chinese craftsmen. The
thread which takes the
weight off the ear is just
visible running diagonally
across the hair from the top
of the hoop. Notice the
braids starting at the level of
the ears.

84. Man's amulet box, *ga'u chengap*
Silver and silver-gilt, eastern Tibet, *c.*20th century
22.7 cm high, 17.2 cm wide, 7.5 cm deep

This amulet box exemplifies the embossing technique of eastern Tibet which shows a greater precision and sharpness than work from other regions (cf. plates 61, 62). By comparing variations in the style of scrollwork, and certain symbols such as the 'Eight Auspicious Emblems' and the monster mask, both shown here, it is often possible to locate the region of origin of large *ga'u*s. Such styles are identifiable as central/southern and eastern Tibetan, Bhutanese, Newari and Chinese.[20] The scrollwork on this piece is typical of eastern Tibet in its consistency, showing little space between tendrils (cf. plate 62 from Lhasa). Not only are the auspicious emblems on eastern Tibetan pieces more detailed and three dimensional than those from other areas, but several are totally different in form. The heads of the fish in the 'Two fish' symbol here for example meet at the bottom while on *ga'u* from central/southern Tibet (plates 61, 62) their bodies arch together with heads meeting at the top.
© The British Museum

85. Amulet box, *ga'u*
Iron
Probably eastern Tibet, *c.*17th century
8.5 cm long, 9cm wide, 2.7 cm deep

The front of the box is composed of pierced ironwork scrolls incorporating the 'Eight Auspicious Emblems', dragons and clouds. Iron is seldom used to make amulet containers probably because, compared to gold or silver, it is not usually valued as a material for ornaments. It also has additional negative associations with blacksmiths, traditionally among the lowest in Tibetan society and with rituals such as exorcism (page 30). However, as texts say it frightens hungry ghosts and evil spirits, it might be thought most suitable for warding off negative spiritual forces.
National Museums Liverpool

86. **MAN'S AMULET BOX**, *ga'u chengap* (FORMERLY OWNED BY SURKHANG SHAPÉ)
Silver and silver-gilt
Eastern Tibet,
*c.*20th century
28.5 cm high

A finely worked *ga'u* decorated with the 'Eight Offering Goddesses' set amidst scrollwork. Very large box *ga'u* such as this were only worn, or carried by one's servants, as protection on long journeys. While travelling they could be set up as temporary shrines during stops en route but at other times would be kept on the family altar. The abbots of monasteries and other high-ranking religious figures commissioned box *ga'u*s as lavish as any nobleman's[21] which, when not in use, were displayed on their private altars.
Ashmolean Museum, Oxford

# Western Tibet, Ladakh, Bhutan and Sikkim

87. WOMEN'S HEAD ORNAMENTS, modelled in 2003
Silver, enamel, turquoise, coral and turquoise, c.mid 20th century
Rongchung district, Ngari, western Tibet

The jewellery of women in Ngari is amongst the most elaborate in Tibet and is seen to full effect in this set.

A turquoise-covered *perak* headdress is combined with a large silver forehead ornament featuring the sun/moon, the symbol of enlightenment, fringed with thin leaves or *genshung*. The latter was only worn down on the most important occasions, at other times it could be flipped back over the head. Framing the face on each side and above are Indian enamelled ear ornaments with attached streamers and bells (see plate 92). As in Kinnaur, Lahaul and Spiti the front edges of the shawl are joined by a lozenge shaped clasp or *digra*.
V&A: IS 10–23–1999

88. SIDE VIEW OF WOMEN'S HEAD ORNAMENTS, modelled in 2003
Silver, enamel, turquoise, coral and turquoise
Rongchung district, Ngari, western Tibet, c.mid 20th century

Large circular ear ornaments add further richness to the ensemble. They hook up at each side to a cotton band that encircles the head.
V&A: IS 10–23–1999

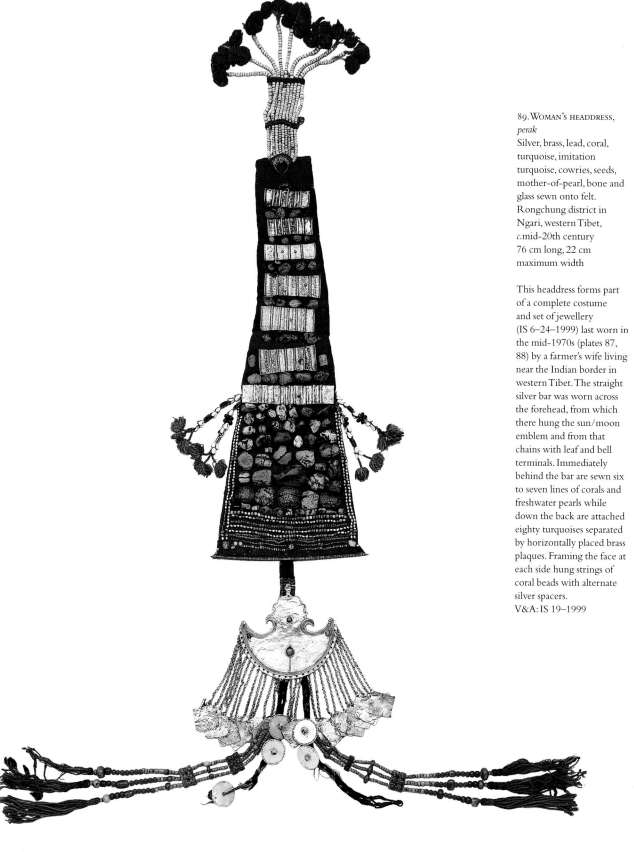

**89. WOMAN'S HEADDRESS,
*perak***
Silver, brass, lead, coral,
turquoise, imitation
turquoise, cowries, seeds,
mother-of-pearl, bone and
glass sewn onto felt.
Rongchung district in
Ngari, western Tibet,
*c.*mid-20th century
76 cm long, 22 cm
maximum width

This headdress forms part
of a complete costume
and set of jewellery
(IS 6–24–1999) last worn in
the mid-1970s (plates 87,
88) by a farmer's wife living
near the Indian border in
western Tibet. The straight
silver bar was worn across
the forehead, from which
there hung the sun/moon
emblem and from that
chains with leaf and bell
terminals. Immediately
behind the bar are sewn six
to seven lines of corals and
freshwater pearls while
down the back are attached
eighty turquoises separated
by horizontally placed brass
plaques. Framing the face at
each side hung strings of
coral beads with alternate
silver spacers.
V&A: IS 19–1999

90. AMULET CASES, *ga'us,*
SHAWL CLASP, BANGLES
Silver and turquoise
Part of a woman's costume
IS 6–24–1999
Rongchung district in
Ngari, western Tibet,
*c.*mid-20th century

Rectangular amulet,
9 cm long, 8.6 cm wide
Cylindrical amulet,
12 cm long, diam. 3 cm
Clasp, 11.5 cm long,
7.5 cm wide
Bracelets, 8.5 cm
maximum width

The rectangular *ga'u* is a
shape often seen in western
and southern Tibet. It was
worn around the neck with
the cylindrically shaped
amulet box called *chugsung,*
full of rolled prayers on
paper, immediately below
it. The lozenge-shaped
silver clasp, or *digra,* set with
turquoise held together the
two front ends of the felt
shawl at the chest.
Accompanying these pieces
are a pair of hollow silver
bracelets, or *dhugu,*
decorated with long-life
(*c.shou*) designs.
Rectangular amulet,
V&A: IS 17–1999
Cylindrical amulet,
V&A: IS 18–1999
Clasp, V&A: IS 14–1999
Bracelets, V&A: IS 20/21–
1999

91. EAR ORNAMENTS, *kontak*
AND FINGER RINGS
Silver, coral and turquoise
Part of a woman's costume;
V&A: IS 6–24–1999.
Rongchung district in
Ngari, western Tibet,
*c*.mid-20th century
Ear ornaments, diam.circles
10 cm, chains 28 cm long
Rings,V&A: IS 11–1999
diam.1.5 cm;V&A: IS
12–1999 diam. 2 cm

This pair of strangely
elegant ear ornaments are
suspended by crescent-
shaped hooks from a cotton
headband encircling the
head.The longest of the sets
of meshed wire chains
hangs towards the front of
the face and the edge of the
circular ear ornament with
corals and turquoise faces
the front. Either side of the
stones, coiled silver wire
decorates and gives body to
the ear ornaments.Two
coral and turquoise inlaid
finger rings lie between
them.
Ear ornaments,
V&A: IS 22/23–1999
Finger rings,
V&A: IS 11/12–1999

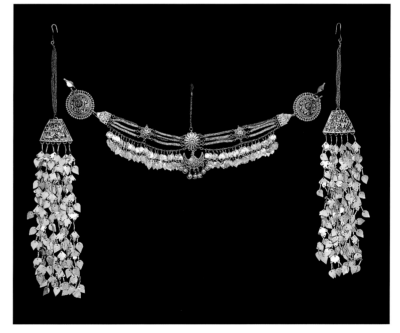

92.WOMEN'S HEAD
ORNAMENTS
Silver and enamel
Part of a woman's costume;
V&A: IS 6–24–1999
Rongchung district in
Ngari, western Tibet,
*c*.mid-20th century

Forehead ornament,
41 cm maximum length
Ear ornaments,
44 cm maximum length,
diam. of disks 4.5 cm

A forehead ornament and
triangular ear ornaments, or
*mulmento,* of silver and
characteristic blue and
green *champlevé* enamel
from the enamel-making
centre of Nurpur in Kangra
district.The forehead
ornament with parallel rows
of silver chains, enamelled
disks and a central crescent
moon hung with bells is
similar to the *daoni tilak*
made in nearby Mandi
(Himachal Pradesh). Both
sets of ornaments support
bunches of silver chains
hung with cascading pipal-
leaf shaped pendants.
Proximity to the border and
cross border trade was
responsible for the adoption
of such Indian items as part
of traditional female attire
in Ngari, Spiti, Lahaul and
Kinnaur.[22]
Forehead ornament,
V&A: IS 10–1999
Ear ornaments,
V&A: IS 15 & 16–1999

93. Dress clasp, *pichuk* (Spiti) or *tomukeh* (Lahaul)
Brass and iron
Lahaul, Spiti or Kinnaur, Himachal Pradesh,
*c*.late 19th century
20 cm high, 19 cm wide

A brass dress clasp from the western Himalayas formed of three separate rings symbolizing the 'Three Jewels' of Buddhism. This is a distinct local type used to pin together the ends of a woman's wrapped upper garment at the left shoulder. It is found throughout a zone in the Himalayan borderlands under different names. Its superficial resemblance to a Celtic brooch led earlier scholars to speculate wildly on improbable cross-cultural links.
V&A: IS 4–1954

**94. WOMAN'S NECKLACE**
Silver, coral and glass
imitation coral
Ladakh, Jammu & Kashmir
State, India, *c.*first half of
19th century
22 cm long, 3 cm wide

This is a distinctively
Ladakhi type of necklace
combining several strands of
coral beads with seven small
oval *ga'u*s. The deep red
'corals' at the top are glass
imitations.
Acquired in Darjeeling in
1855. V&A:13068

**95. WOMAN'S NECKLACE**
Silver, coral and turquoise
Ladakh, Jammu & Kashmir
State, India, *c.*first half of
19th century
22 cm long, 3 cm wide

The fashion in Ladakh and
western Tibet for wearing
multiple strands of
necklaces, which can be
traced to the 14th century,
may be responsible for this
type of necklace that
combines two strings of
coral beads with silver
spacers and drops. The
fringe of drops also recalls
Indian necklace fashions
and suggests influence from
there transmitted via much
used trade routes to the
south.
V&A: IS 1858–1883

**96. WOMAN WEARING
FESTIVAL DRESS**
Leh, Ladakh, 1990

A woman's best attire is
dominated by her *perak*
headdress, traditionally
given to the eldest daughter
when she marries. Its
dozens of turquoises may
therefore represent pieces
collected and passed down
over many generations. The
costume is completed by a
chatelaine, hung from the
shoulder, freshwater pearl
earrings, an elaborate
necklace with *ga'u* and a
silver waist ornament with
hanging chains or *dodchas*.
A needle-case and purse
are sometimes added.
Photograph by Graham
Brandon

**97. WOMAN'S WAIST
ORNAMENT,** *dodchas*
**WOMAN'S CHATELAINE SET,**
*sondus*
**WOMAN'S BRACELETS,** *tunglak*
**WOMAN'S HEADDRESS,** *perak*
Silver, brass, turquoise,
coral, cornelian, conch
shell.
Leh, Ladakh, *c*.1930
Waist ornament: 309 cm
long
Chatelaine: 28 cm long
Bracelets: 6 cm diam.
Headdress: 96 cm long,
13 cm maximum width

Parts of a complete set of
female Ladakhi costume and
jewellery. The pierced brass
disk in the form of the luck-
bringing 'Endless Knot' with
streamers of cowry shells,
ending in bell terminals,
hangs at the waist from a tie-
dyed silk waistband. The
other ornaments are a silver
vanity set including

tweezers, nail- and tooth-
pick and brush which is
attached to the left shoulder
(plate 98) and the pair of
conch shell bracelets. These
are placed on the wrists of a
girl when young and cut off
and replaced when
outgrown. They normally
then remain on the wrists
for a woman's whole life.

The headdress was acquired
separately and is the type
worn in Rupshu (eastern
Ladakh) and in adjoining
Ngari (western Tibet) with a
flat bar at the front (plate 89).
Waist ornament, V&A: IS
17d–1989; chatelaine, V&A:
IS 17f–1989; bracelets, V&A:
IS 17b&c1989; headdress,
V&A: IS 7–1954

98. WOMAN WEARING
FESTIVAL DRESS
Leh, Ladakh, 1990 (detail)

The *perak* is a status symbol
for a Ladakhi woman, her
wealth and position are
shown by the number and
quality of the turquoises
present. This is one of the
best *perak* with up to nine
lines of stones and a
maximum width of 25
centimetres, the poorest
might have only one line
and be 10 centimetres wide.
This woman is wearing the

most popular type of
earring composed of strings
of freshwater pearls
attached to a metal hoop
whose weight is supported
by chains. Both the earrings
and her face are framed
against black wool ear flaps
or *tsaru*. Her necklace of
coral, turquoise, pearls and
*dzi* beads combines a
central octagonal *ga'u* and a
turquoise-inlaid 'Wish-
Fulfilling Jewel'.
Photograph by Graham
Brandon

99. BACK OF A WOMAN'S
HEADDRESS, *perak*
Leh, Ladakh, 1990

From above the *perak*
headdress resembles a
snakeskin and from the
front a woman wearing one
is reminiscent of a raised
cobra about to strike, a
resemblance made stronger
by the two black-wool ear
flaps worn at each side of
the head.[23] The snake
imagery is deliberate as
women in Ladakh are
traditionally associated with
the *lu*, the underworld
spirits of the waters.[24] The

wealthiest women have a
further side decoration of
up to ten strings of coral
beads hung from a silver bar
down the back on the left
side. The sides of the head
are enriched with hanging
silver ornaments, or *shunga*,
in the form of silver plaques
or auspicious knot motifs,
from which hang small
bells. Along the sides of the
head hang silver chain
ornaments, or *daoni*,
imported from Mandi in
Himachal Pradesh.[25]
Photograph by Graham
Brandon.

101. CHATELAINE ORNAMENT
Silver, turquoise and garnet
Acquired in Sikkim
Possibly western Himalayas,
*c.*19th century
14 cm diam., 4 cm high

This convex silver
ornament is covered with
concentric circles of
turquoise, garnet and
filigree. Although the
turquoise points to Tibetan
taste, other aspects of the
piece such as its ring of
garnets, symmetrical filigree
work and beaded outer
edge are Indian in style.
This suggests that it
originated in an area where
mixed cultures prevailed
such as Sikkim or another
sub–Himalayan area. Its
back is fitted with three
loops for attachment to a
belt or garment.[26]
Bequest of Lord Curzon.
V&A: IM 162–1927

100. PAIR OF BRACELETS,
*dobchu*
Silver, turquoise, glass
imitation turquoise, coral
Probably eastern Bhutan,
*c.*first half of the 19th
century
6.5 cm maximum diam.
2.3 cm width of band

This type of heavy silver
bangle was popular in the
eastern part of the kingdom
of Bhutan and in related
forms in Tibet. Their
surfaces are encrusted with
pearled and plaited wire
and silver granulation. The
small ill fitting stones which
are probably replacements
are imitations.
Obtained in Sikkim and
acquired by the East India
Company Museum in
1855. V&A: 03468&a

102. MAN'S AMULET BOX
Silver and woven cotton
Bhutan, 19th century
14 cm high, 11 cm wide,
6.4 cm deep

A beautifully embossed box *ga'u* made by Bhutanese craftsmen who traditionally imitated eastern Tibetan forms of scrollwork and auspicious emblems. Their own scrollwork, seen here, achieved a similar depth and clarity of detail but was slightly thicker and more overlapping in form. The first Political Officer, Sikkim and Bhutan, John Claude White (in office 1889–1908) was particularly impressed by Bhutanese metalwork. He attributed its excellence to the fact that craftsmen were kept on retaining fees by district governors, giving them abundant time to spend on individual orders.
National Museums
Liverpool

103. DRESS PINS, *tinkhup*, AND ROUND CLIPS, *koma*
Silver, silver-gilt, imitation glass, turquoise
Bhutan, 19th and 20th centuries
Large dress pins:
38.5 cm (chain lengths)
Round clips:
48.2 cm overall length, each clasp 5.1 cm wide
Small dress pins: 16 cm long, ring diam. 5 cm

The changing styles of shoulder pins/clips used in Bhutan over the last century to join the women's garment (*kira*) are charted here. Up until the start of the 20th century two cumbersome silver swivel pins or *tinkhup* balanced by chains which lay across the back, were the main type in use. Smaller versions of these came in sometime at the start of the 20th century and soon began to include attached round plaques. The two round plaques were then produced on their own without the pins and are worn today with an interconnecting chain at the front of the body. The examples shown here are decorated with auspicious 'Endless Knot' designs.

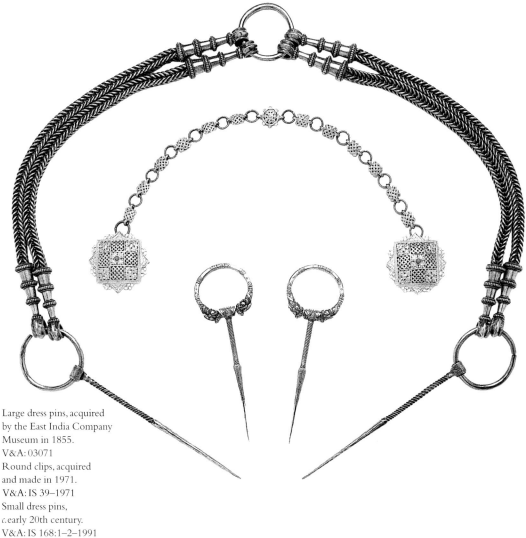

Large dress pins, acquired by the East India Company Museum in 1855.
V&A: 03071
Round clips, acquired and made in 1971.
V&A: IS 39–1971
Small dress pins, *c.*early 20th century.
V&A: IS 168:1–2–1991

# Nepal

104. TWO PAIRS OF
BRACELETS, N.*sinkhwa
lun churi*
Copper-gilt
Nepal, *c.*first half of 19th
century
03009&a: 11 cm diam.
03011&a: 8 cm diam.

The usual form of Newar
bracelets with facing

dragon-head terminals, a
type also worn in Tibet. On
the larger hollow pair a
section of the ring hinges
out to allow fitting to the
arm. The smaller pieces are
solid cast.
Acquired by the East India
Company Museum in
1855. V&A: 03009&a,
03011&a

105. PAIR OF EARRINGS,
N. *dhungri*
Gold
Probably Middle Hills,
Nepal, *c.*18th/19th century
4.2 cm square

A square form of the more
usually round *dhungri*
earring once worn by the
Indo-Nepalese and Tibeto-
Burman peoples of the
Middle Hills. A square
earring, with a similar
pattern of symmetrical
embossed foliage, is shown
being worn on the diagonal
by a 16th- or 17th-century
image of a Bodhisattva in a
Paris collection.[27]
Obtained in Kathmandu;
acquired by the East India
Company Museum in
1855. V&A: IS 08672

106. WOMAN'S NECK
ORNAMENT, N. *tayo*
Copper-gilt, silk thread
Obtained in Kathmandu,
Nepal, *c.*first half of 19th
century
Lozenge pendant:
12 cm long

An important piece of
Newar ceremonial
jewellery which has
protective functions such as
guarding against evil spirits.
It is considered essential for
a bride and is also used in
the ceremonies prior to
menstruation and on
entering old age. Although
hollow, it is closed and
cannot be used as an amulet
container. Its cylindrical
form suggests an Indian
origin as does the tear-drop
ornament on the upper
edge recalling the double-
mango motif on Indian
jewellery. *Tayo* are also worn
by dancers depicting deities
(plate 107)
Acquired by the East India
Company Museum in
1855. V&A: IS 03034

107. Two boys dressed as deities in a procession
Kathmandu, early 1980s

The boy at the front of the picture is dressed as Krishna, an incarnation of Vishnu, and wears a crown, *tayo* neck ornament, armlets and cuff bracelets. Behind him is another boy portraying Radha, Krishna's wife, with a gold chain hair ornament, or *nyapu sikha*, normally worn by girls. Photograph by Hannelore Gabriel

**108. FOREHEAD ORNAMENT FOR AN IMAGE**
*Jarao* work
Silver-gilt, turquoise, coral, lapis lazuli, (mixed-cut) rubies, (mixed-cut) sapphires, (rose-cut) diamonds, (step and mixed-cut) aquamarine, zircon and freshwater pearls.
Kathmandu Valley in Nepal or Tibet, *c.*18th century
22 cm long, 6.5 cm wide

The gently curving convex plaque was intended to fit the forehead of a large image, attaching to the crown by two hooks at the side. Carved corals and turquoises are used to represent three crowned meditational Buddhas. At the centre is the red Amitabha and at either side the blue Akshobya. The wide variety of precious stones and their disparate cuts suggests they were gathered from many sources over a long period of time. Examination also shows that the colour of some of the rubies and aquamarines has been artificially enhanced by placing coloured resin behind them within foil backings.
Purchased from Imre Schwaiger. V&A: IM 160–1913

**109. PAIR OF EARRINGS FOR A RELIGIOUS IMAGE**
*Jarao* work
Silver, silver-gilt, turquoise, lapis lazuli, coral, pearl, feldspar, zircons, pink and blue sapphires, aquamarines, emeralds and diamonds.
Kathmandu Valley in Nepal or Tibet, *c.*18th century
7.5 cm square, 1.5 cm thick

These heavy earrings were clearly intended for attachment to a large image. Both plaques have foiled diamonds at their centres and a field of gems enclosed within a border of turquoise lotus petals. Four coral monster masks are placed in each corner.
V&A: IM 89&90–1911

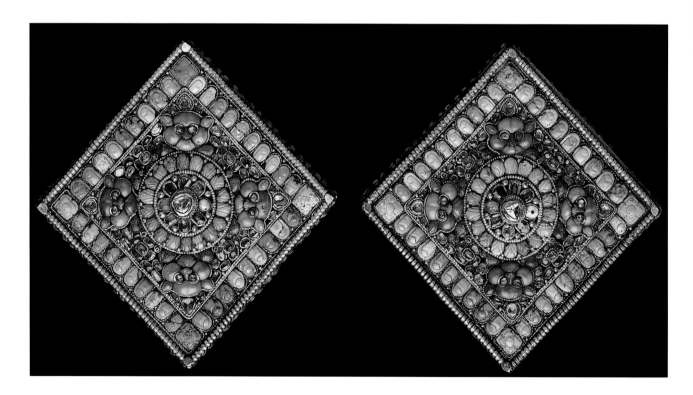

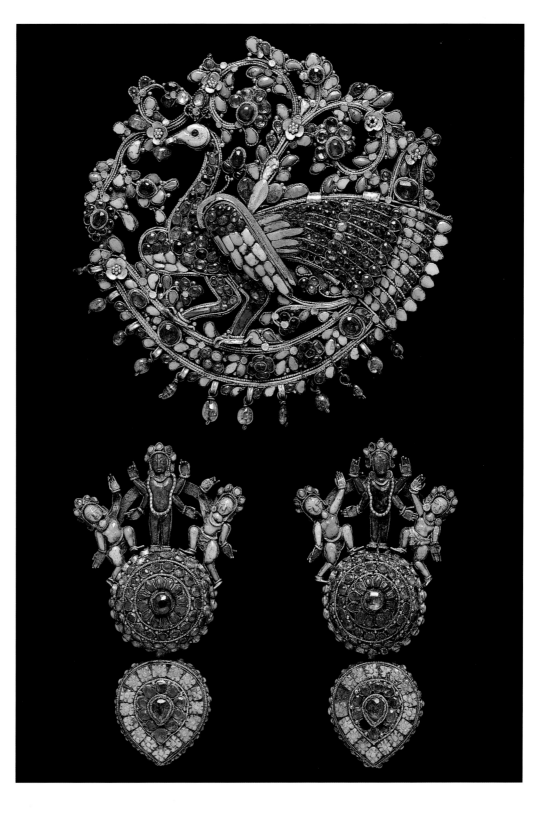

**110. Set of ceremonial jewellery**
Silver-gilt, turquoise, coral, spinels, beryl, rubies, sapphires, diamonds, hessonite garnet, and lapis lazuli.
Kathmandu Valley, Nepal, *c.*17th or 18th century
13 cm square, 2 cm thick
Ceremonial Earrings
Silver-gilt, turquoise, lapis lazuli with foiled rubies and sapphires
Kathmandu Valley, Nepal, *c.*17th or 18th century.
11 cm long, 6 cm wide, 3.5 cm deep

This set of ceremonial jewellery shows the Newar stone carving and setting tradition at its height. A gracefully portrayed peacock forms the centre of an openwork design of tendrils and clusters of flowers depicted in metal and settings of precious stones. The peacock is a symbol of luck, prosperity and longevity for both Hindus and Buddhists and is deified as Maha-Mayuri, the Great Peacock.
The earrings show two attendant figures each side of a four-armed deity whose deep blue colour suggests that it may be Vishnu.
National Museums of Scotland

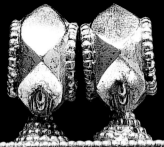

111. CEREMONIAL AMULET
BOX, N.*jantar*
*Jarao* work
Silver-gilt, turquoise, coral,
(mixed-cut) rubies, (mixed-
cut) sapphires, (oval, step
and mixed-cut) emeralds
and (oval mixed-cut)
hessonite garnets
Kathmandu Valley, Nepal
*c.*18th century
9.2 cm high, 7.6 cm wide,
1.5 cm deep

The central symbol is the
Nepalese version of the
Tibetan monster mask,
N.*chepu,* whose horned
face and two hands grasping
foliage is skilfully
represented using carved
turquoises which are also
used to form a lotus-petal
edge to the box. Above the
head is the 'Wish-Fulfilling
Jewel' formed from two
emeralds and a ruby. The
fashion for using this
distinctively Newari type of
stone inlay called *jarao* or
*jadoba* (page 60) was
strongest during the 18th
and 19th centuries. The
technique uses a network of
cloisons formed from thin
strips of wire to hold
stones, often combined as
here, with spiral filigree
elements. In Nepal it
appears from as early as the
12th century where it
decorates the front of the
ritual crowns worn by
priests.[28]
V&A: IM 91–1911

112. BELT CLASP
*Jarao* work
Silver and silver-gilt,
turquoise, white and red
coral, amber, (cabouchon
and mixed-cut) spinels and
rubies, (mixed-cut)
sapphires, (cabouchon and
mixed-cut) emeralds (oval
mixed-cut), white topaz
Kathmandu Valley, Nepal,
*c.*18th century
15 cm long, 6 cm wide

The central panel of this
three-part clasp bears the
emblem of the S.*visvavajra*
or crossed *vajra*,
representing the
unshakeable stability of the
enlightened state. At its
centre is a single white
topaz. Monster masks,
N.*chepu,* formed of carved
coral and turquoise guard
each end. *Jarao* stone inlay
of this type was used to
decorate a wide variety of
ornaments, shrines, ritual
objects and sword and knife
hilts. When the tourist
market first developed in
the 1960s, it became
popular as a decoration for
trinket boxes and decorative
animal figures. But after
reaching a peak of
production in the 1970s, it
declined rapidly and today
is found only on tourist
jewellery and Christmas
decorations.
V&A: IS 43–1962

113. CEREMONIAL NECKLACE,
N.*suta* OR *konchi*
Copper-gilt, turquoise,
coral, rubies, (mixed-cut)
sapphires
Kathmandu Valley, Nepal
*c.*19th century
24 cm high with pendants,
10 cm wide

A wide gorget necklace
with a central plaque of
pale pink coral carved into
the form of the deity
Ganesh, flanked on either
side by dragons grasping
rubies in each front claw.
The *suta* necklace is often
placed around the necks of
religious images but also
used in the initiation
ceremonies of Newar boys
and girls. *Suta* made for
images usually curve
around the neck while
those such as this, intended
for human wear, are
crescentic and provided
with a chain or cord. This is
an ancient form which can
be traced back at least as far
as the 9th century in the art
of north India.
V&A: IM 296–1913

**114. PAIR OF EARRINGS**
Silver, copper-gilt, glass and
seed pearls
Kathmandu Valley, Nepal
c.18th or 19th century.
4.5 cm diameter

Constructed in alternate
concentric circles of silver-
gilt petals and imitation
sapphires, rubies and
emeralds forming open
lotuses, edged with seed
pearls. The very large posts
for attachment at the back
of each indicates that they
were probably intended for
the ears of an image.
V&A: IM 149&a–1910

**115. EARRING**
Silver, silver-gilt, lapis lazuli,
turquoise, seed pearls, ruby,
emeralds
Kathmandu Valley, Nepal
c.18th or 19th century
10–5 cm high, 5.5 cm wide

A tiny but beautifully made
standing figure of the
mythical half-man, half-
eagle Garuda, the vehicle
of the Hindu deity Vishnu.
Garuda is also a frequently
encountered protective
emblem in Buddhist
culture. A peacock-like fan
of tail feathers with
turquoises at their tips rises
at the back of the head.
The lower edge is hung
with seed pearls and small
leaves of silver-gilt.
Purchased from Imre
Schwaiger. V&A: IM
181–1913

116. CEREMONIAL NECKLACE, N.*toh*
Copper-gilt, lapis lazuli, turquoise, coral and blue enamel
Kathmandu Valley, Nepal, 18th or 19th century

A collar worn by both boys and girls in childhood initiation rituals. The presence of markedly Chinese-style dragons, and the use of enamelling surrounding the cabouchon turquoises and corals which is not traditional in Nepal, is puzzling. Could Newars living in Tibet or even Mongolia have picked up Chinese designs and techniques, or might the Chinese delegations which visited Nepal in the 19th century be responsible for such long-distance influence? A number of similar pieces have been photographed in use in Nepal during the late 1970s.[29] More recent examples are plainer and may be flat rather than round.
© The British Museum

117. EARRING FOR IMAGE
Silver-gilt, turquoise, lapis
lazuli, beryl, spinels, coral
pink and blue sapphires.
Kathmandu Valley,
Nepal or Tibet,
*c.*18th or 19th century
14 cm high, 5 cm wide

One of a pair of heavy
earrings made for
attachment to an image.
The top roundel contains
the typically fat-cheeked
style of the Newar monster
mask, or *chepu,* with two
hands and facial features
outlined in thin wire and
with inset stone eyes. The
'Wish-Fulfilling Jewel'
appears above the creature's
head. The lowest plaque
bears the peacock, a
favourite Newar emblem,
believed to neutralize
poison and guard against
death from snakebite.
Purchased from Imre
Schwaiger. V&A: IM
84a–1911

# Notes

## Preface

[1] Weihreter, H., *Schmuck aus dem Himalaja*, 1978; Windisch Graetz, S & G, *Juwelen des Himalaya*, 1981.
[2] Jones, 1996, Reynolds, 1999, and Untracht in *Traditional Jewellery of India*, 1997.

## Chapter 1

[1] Heller, 1999, pp.7-52.
[2] Probably called *Tsug* in the 7th to 9th centuries.
[3] It has been estimated that at least one million Tibetans have lost their life.
[4] Created by the collision of two tectonic plates 50 million years ago.
[5] At up to 5,500 metres.
[6] Bhutan and Sikkim are well known as rice-producing areas from which in the past rice was exported to Tibet. Sikkim's name, *dre jong*, means 'rice country'.
[7] Rizvi, 1998, p.56, Shakya, 1982, p.16.
[8] Aris, 1979, pp.57-59.
[9] Kotturan, 1983, pp.30-31, Steinmann, 1998, pp.121-122.
[10] Gabriel, 1999, p.109, settling in the regions of Solu Khumbu and Helambu.
[11] Myers and Bean, 1994, pp.47-48.
[12] Shakya, 1982, p.16, Rizvi, 1998, p.54.
[13] Raha and Mahato, 1895, pp.295-296, 299.
[14] At 2,500 to 4,500 metres.
[15] Heller, 1999, p.55, Rizvi, 1998, pp. 65,68,73.
[16] Warikoo, 1989, pp.55-89, Rizvi, 1998, pp.98-112.
[17] The Akshi Chin.
[18] T. *Dromo* 'wheat land'.

## Chapter 2

[1] Sakya & Emery, 1990, p.3.
[2] Yeshi, Pugh, Phipps, 1992, p.76, Yuthok, 1995, p.188.
[3] Untracht, 1997, p.146, fig. 259, p.155, fig. 275.
[4] Belleza, 1998, p.60 illus.59 for Bon *ga'u*.
[5] Sakya & Emery, 1990, p.306.
[6] Reynolds, 1999, p.99, plate 39.
[7] Reynolds, 1999, p.99.
[8] Clarke, 1995, vol.1, p.128, Singer, 1996, p.21 footnote 33.
[9] Yuthok, 1995, p.186.
[10] Singer, 1996, p.20.
[11] Clarke 1995, vol.1, p.127.
[12] Yeshe, Pugh, Phipps, 1992, pp.79-80.
[13] Khenrap, 2000, p.73, both sets were also sometimes provided by the groom's family.
[14] Bell, 1928 repr.1991, p.180.
[15] Goldstein, 2001, p.1013.
[16] Yuthok, 1995, p.322, Jones, 1996, p.276.
[17] Kawaguchi, 1909, p.360, MacDonald, 1929, p.138.
[18] Personal communication from Monisha Ahmed, July 2002.
[19] Bell, 1928 repr.1991, p.164.
[20] In the Water Ox Year, translation by Michael Henss.
[21] Heller, 2003, pp.55-57.
[22] Rockhill, 1894, pp.357-358.
[23] Nieuhof, 1673, p.358, Govinda, 1979, vol.2, pp. 119, 189.
[24] Beall, 1989, pp. 57, 101, Normantas, 1994, pp. 9, 37.
[25] Klimburg Salter, 1997, p.94, figs.55, 56, p.125, fig.123.
[26] Goepper & Poncar, 1996, pp.79, 137, 143, Pal, 1984, pl.17, 13th-century *tangka* showing same.
[27] Yule, 1913, p.150.
[28] Untracht, 1997, p.211, pl. 427, Weihreter, 1988, p.197, pls.114, 249, 273, in Lahaul called *mulang* or *kirkirtsi*.
[29] Rockhill, 1891, p.76.
[30] Richardson, 1993, pp.14-17, Singer, 1996, pp.21-22.
[31] Reynolds, 1999, p. 84, Clarke, 2001, pp.46-47.
[32] Reynolds, 1999, p.84, Shanghai Museum, 2000, p.165, pl.77.
[33] Clarke, 2001, pp.46-47.
[34] Singer, 1999, pp.173-174.
[35] Henss, 1996, p.213, Heller, 2001, p.70.
[36] Heller, 1999, p.35, illus.26.
[37] Indian Museum, Calcutta: images 3803/A25141, Kr 7.
[38] Haarh, 1969, p.314, the closed *ga'u* as the primeval source of life, in the colophon.
[39] Bellezza, 1998, pp.44-64.
[40] Yuthok, 1995, p.321.
[41] Personal communication from Monisha Ahmed, July 2002.
[42] Yuthok, 1995, pp.187-188. Dorje Yudon Yuthok's memories of life in Lhasa stretched back to before 1920 and her mother and grandmother's recollections went back into the previous century.
[43] Mullin/Wangyal, 1983, pp.10, 19, Yeshi, Pugh, Phipps, 1992, p.81.
[44] Teague, 1995, p.79.
[45] Weihreter, 1988, pp.111, 113, Gabriel, 1995, pp. 90-95.
[46] Klimburg-Salter, 1997, p.94, figs.55-56, p.125, fig.123, Heller, 2001, p.70.
[47] Rockhill, 1895, p.690.

## Chapter 3

[1] Huxley, 1954.
[2] Conze, 1959, pp.222-223, 232-233 the *Sukhavativyuha*, 'Description of the Happy Land'.
[3] Beer, 1999, p.210.
[4] Dagyab, 1995, pp.70-71, Beer, 1999, p.162, for its beneficial worldly properties.
[5] Snodgrass, 1985, pp. 213-214.
[6] Guenther, 1989.
[7] Parfionovitch, 1992, p.61.
[8] Ebbinghouse and Winsten, 1988, pp.45-46, 48 for legends.

9 Stein, in Macdonald 1971, pp. 232, 305, 505, 509, Heller, 1986, p.76.

10 Pogue, 1915, p.114.

11 Richtsfeld, 1983, p. 306.

12 Vitali, 1996, p. 519.

13 Pogue, 1915, pp. 77, 81.

14 Parfionovitch, 1992, p.217.

15 Laufer,1913, pp. 6, 11, Singer, 1996, p.33, Bell, 1928 repr.1991, pp.151, 240.

16 Walker-Watson, 1983, pp.16, 17, Untracht,1997, p.145, Gabriel, 1999, pp.56-57.

17 Snodgrass, 1985, p.351, Untracht, 1997, p.145.

18 Parfionovitch, 1992, p.217.

19 Weihreter, 1988, p.22.

20 Singer, 1996, p.33.

21 Parfionovitch, 1992, p.61.

22 Clarke, 1995, pp. 64–65.

23 Beer, 1999, p.215.

24 Yeshi (ed.), 1987, p.80, Beer, 1999, p.215.

25 Singer, 1996, pp.12-13, Beer, 1999, p.215.

26 Woodford Schmidt, 1995, pp.16-33. Amulets worn by 10th- and 11th-century stone images display tiger-claw amulets a type still worn in the 20th century, see Untracht, 1997, pp.91-96.

27 Olson, 1950, vol.2, p.55, Beer, 1999, p.161, Untracht, 1997, pp.91-96.

28 Olson, 1950, vol.2, p.56, Beer, 1999, p.161.

29 Czuma, 1978, figs. 3 & 5 for Jain prototypes, Beer, 1999, pp.171-172.

30 Dagyab,1995, pp.17, 115.

31 Salter, 1982, p.139, pls. 61, 69, 73, Whitfield, 1982-85, vol.2, fig 78.

32 For the full set see Dagyab, 1995, pp.15-36, Reynolds, 1999, pp.255-6.

33 Written *dzi bar* but commonly pronounced as *zibag*. The name is a transliteration of the Sanskrit name *cipata*, meaning 'flat nosed'.

34 Singer, 1996, pp.40-41, Beer, 1999, p.69.

**Chapter 4**

1 Schafer, 1963, pp. 222, 230, 232-333.

2 Heron, 1930, p.27, Schafer, 1963, p.231.

3 Haarh, 1969, pp. 350, 388.

4 Haarh, 1969, p.347, the *Dro* clan, Heller, 1998, pp.86-87, fig.6.

5 Markham, 1879, p.100.

6 Lo Bue, 1981, p.58.

7 Markham, 1879, p.100.

8 Aluminium phosphate.

9 Stein, 1971, p.509.

10 Laufer, 1913, pp.17-18, Walker-Watson, 1983, p.16.

11 Aitchison, 1874, pp.85, 164, Laufer, 1913, pp. 17, 19-20.

12 Pogue, 1915, pp.12-14, 34, 40, 71-72, Heron, 1930, p.26.

13 Aitchinson, 1874, p. 85.

14 Ramsay, 1886, pp.162–163, Laufer, 1913, pp.18-19.

15 Pogue, 1915, p.82 footnote 10, Wilson, 1997/98, p.34.

16 Waddell, 1906, p.348.

17 Yule, 1926, p.49.

18 Del Mare, 1996, pp.10-13 and illus.

19 Gerard 1841, pp. 183, 297-298, Aitchison, 1874, p.164.

20 Aitchison, 1874, p.164, Yogev, 1978, pp.102-105.

21 Stephens, 1985, p.21.

22 Migot, 1955, p.94, Parmee, 1972, p.81.

23 Untracht, 1997, p.147.

24 Yogev, 1978, pp.104, 108, Rice, 1980, pp. 20, 57.

25 Tavernier, 1977 repr. vol.3, pp.203, 208.

26 Migot, 1955, p.243, Ronge, 1978, p.144.

27 Aaronson, 2001, pp.131–132, 200.

28 Camman, 1952, p.163, Untracht, 1997, p.333.

29 Probably Italian coral imported to nearby Fort St George (Madras).

30 Clarke, 1998, pp.52-54, 64-65.

31 Aitchison, 1874, p.300.

32 Boyer, 1952, p.175, Aaronson, 2001, p.144.

33 Boyer, 1952, p.175, Camman, 1951, p.60, Schafer, 1963, p.244.

34 Aaronson, 2001, pp.146, 157, 161, 178-179.

35 Hornell, 1914, pp. 3 f, 69,75, Yule & Burnell, 1996 repr., p.184.

36 Liu, 1995, p.224.

37 Camman, 1951, pp.162-163.

38 Emerald is a beryl coloured green by chromium and vanadium or both.

39 Untracht, 1997, p.328.

40 Finot, 1896, p.41, Hughes, 1997, p.304.

41 Grenard, 1904, p.300, Hughes, 1997, pp. 280, 286.

42 Heron, 1930, p.27.

43 Lo Bue, 1985/86, p. 412.

44 Van Spengen, 2000, p.127.

45 Lo Bue, 1981, pp. 54, 57, Singer, 1996, p.32.

46 Singer, 1996, p.32.

47 Vitali, 1996, p.329.

48 Ronge, 1978, p.144, Lo Bue, 1981, p.54.

49 Trotter, 1877, p.102, Wakefield, 1966, p.42.

50 Lo Bue, 1981, p.56.

51 Lo Bue, 1981, p.56-57.

52 Lo Bue, 1981, p.53.

53 Lo Bue, 1981, p.44, Warikoo, 1989, pp.77, 82, 85.

54 Lo Bue, 1981, p.53.

55 Wojkowitz, 1952, p.132.

56 Ebbinghouse & Winsten, 1988, pp.47-49.

57 Ebbinghouse & Winsten, 1988, pp. 39-40, white lead and potash can also be used.

58 Untracht, 1997, p.148.

59 Jones, 1996, p.308.

**Chapter 5**

1 For Lahaul see Mamgain, 1975, p.127, for Spiti, see Harcourt, 1874, p.76, Mamgain,1975, p.157, for Kinnaur see Sharma, 1967, p.46, for Ladakh see Clarke, 1998, pp. 9-18, Clarke, 1999, pp.58-71.

2 Clarke, 1995, vol.1, pp.9-18.

3 Rockhill, 1891, p.81, Rockhill, 1894, p.115, Rockhill, 1895, p.708.

4 In 1952 they were gathered together at *Dechen Choling* to assist with the building of a new palace.

5 Tucci, 1978, pp.150-151.

6 Gill, 1883, p.136, Macdonald, 1929, p.235.

7 Clarke, 1995, vol.1, p.112, Singer, 1996, p.36.

[8] Clarke, 2002, pp.122-125.

[9] Due to a tax imposed by the government workshop on each skill practised by freelance workers.

[10] Teague, 1995, p.50.

[11] Clarke, 2002, pp.122-125.

[12] Huc, 1928, repr. vol.2, p.182, Ronge, 1978, pp.87, 129, Lo Bue, 1985/86, p.409, Clarke, 2002, pp.120-122, 126-127.

[13] Clarke, 1995: vol.1, p.116.

[14] Schweizer, 1976, p.93.

[15] Yuthok, 1995, p.190.

[16] Ju Mipham, 1993, p.103, AL5, quoting from Ratna Lingpa's 'rta dmar las tshogs'.

[17] Dagyab, 1977, vol.1, p.49, sa tshur nag po, Untracht, 1997, p.145, fig.257 for another recipe.

[18] In Ladakh a citric acid solution made from local apricots is used, in east Tibet in the past a solution was made from a seed ta bu and sulphur.

[19] Dagyab, 1977, p.48.

[20] Dagyab, 1977, p.48, the red dye is called rgyam tshal dmarpo, see Dilmar Geshe bzo gnas for a similar recipe using lam ber, laccha, pine resin, soot and kaolin.

[21] See Rauber Schweizer, 1976, pp.148-149 for detailed names.

[22] See Rauber Schweizer, 1976, p.146, 'jur mig.

[23] Simple rounded iron rockers with rounded blades are used in Bhutan while the Chinese in eastern Tibet also use a manufactured threading device which is wound around the wire.

[24] Sodium tetraborate.

[25] Though alloys and casting processes used in making religious images do feature see Lo Bue, 1981.

[26] Two scholars, De'u dmar (dGe bshes) bstan 'dzin phun tshogs also called Dilmar Geshe, (born 1672) and 'Jam mgon 'Ju Mipham rgya mtsho (1846-1912) in their bzo gnas texts both quote passages from Ratna Ling pa's rTa dmar las tshog. 'Ju Mipham acknowledges his debt, Dilmar Geshe does not.

[27] Dilmar Geshe, 1990, pp.71-72. 'Ju Mipham, 1993, p.103, AL5 ff.

[28] Das, 1960, p.917, 'ba'.

## Chapter 6

[1] Teague, 1995, p.122.

[2] Usually ruby, pearl, diamond, emerald, tiger's eye, topaz, sapphire, zircon and coral.

[3] Gabriel, 1999, p.17, although this is not the case in modern Nepalese law.

[4] Teague, 1995, p.276.

[5] Gabriel, 1999, p.21.

[6] Gabriel, 1999, p.27.

[7] Teague, 1995, pp.276-277.

[8] Pal, 1988, vol.2, pp.125, 164, 174, 208.

[9] Schroeder, 1981, pp.313, 343, 355-59, Uhlig, 1995, pp.135, 152.

[10] MacDonald and Stahl, 1979, p.150, Gabriel, 1999, p.25, Bajracharya, 2001, p.77.

[11] Gabriel, 1999, pp.23-25.

[12] See Gabriel, 1999, pp. 75-76.

[13] Gabriel, 1999, p.31.

[14] Lo Bue, 1985, p.262.

[15] Hodgson, 1874, repr. 1971, p.108.

[16] Gabriel, 1999, p.54, rhodolite and almandine garnet.

[17] Gajurel and Vaidya, 1984, pp.57-65, Dhoo meaning 'dust' and sa 'one who handles'.

[18] Gabriel, 1999, p.52.

[19] Teague, 1995, p.78.

[20] Teague, 1995, p.162, a mixture of the resin from Sal trees, mustard seed oil and brick dust.

[21] Stephens, 1985, pp.27-28.

[22] Mukherjee, 1978, p.453, Stephens, 1985, pp.31-32, Teague, 1995, pp.226-7.

[23] Stephens, 1985, pp.30-31.

## Caption Footnotes

[1] Roerich, 1931, p.261.

[2] Roerich, 1931, p.261.

[3] Singer, 1996, pp.116-117, Reynolds, 1999, p.85.

[4] Reynolds, 1978, p.45, Reynolds, 1999, p.99 plate 38.

[5] Yeshi & Phipps, 1992, p.80.

[6] Richardson, 1993, pp.14–17, Reynolds, 1999, p.84, Clarke, 2001, p.467.

[7] Essen and Thingo, 1989, p.295, plate 197, Clarke, 2001, p.467, plate 2.

[8] Singer, 1996, p.21, illustration 46.

[9] Landon, 1928, vol.1, pp. 236-239.

[10] Richardson, 1993, pp.14-17, Singer, 1996, pp.21-22. Reynolds, 1999, p.84, plate 36.

[11] Singer, 1996, p.21 footnote 33.

[12] Schmidt/Thome, 1975, p.114.

[13] Ekvall & Cassinelli, 1969, p.366, communication from Monisha Ahmed, July 2002, on long earring in Ladakh.

[14] Clarke, 1995 vol.1, p.129, vol.2, pp.440-442 illustrated, Untracht, 1999, p.145, dorjema. Stein, 2001, p.202 gru bshi, 'square'.

[15] Yuthok, 1995, pp.185-186, for the 16 types see 321-325.

[16] Singer, 1996, p.20.

[17] Yeshi, Pugh, Phipps, 1992, p.74, Reynolds, 1999, p.88.

[18] Yeshi, Pugh, Phipps, 1992, p.76, Untracht, 1997, p.36 plate 38.

[19] Boyer, 1952, p.192.

[20] For mixed styles and the issue of copying see Clarke, 1997, pp.287-289.

[21] Landon, 1905, vol.1, p.376, illustration of three shrine-shaped ga'us owned by the Regent of Tibet.

[22] Archer, 1986, p.65.

[23] Untracht, 1997, p.152.

[24] Kaplanian, 1981, p.86.

[25] Untracht, 1997, pp.151–152, fig.267.

[26] Jones, 1996, pp.253-254, pls.10, 30, another example.

[27] Macdonald and Stahl, 1979, p.150 pl.111.

[28] Beguin, 1984, p.176.

[29] Windisch Graetz, 1981, pp.167, 171.

# Glossary

*Akor (ae skor)*: lotus-shaped turquoise-covered earring worn by Lhasa women.

*Along (nga long)*: round-hoop earring worn by both sexes in central and southern Tibet. Name of straight earring in eastern Tibet.

*Buti ('bu sgril)*: pearled wire.

*Booga ('bu 'ga)* or *Bubtri (sbub dkris)*: tool for creating the ribbed surface of pearled wire.

*Chagab (rgya gab)*, *Chengab (mchen gab)*: eastern Tibetan names for a man's large amulet box.

*Chorten (mchod rten)*: stepped conical structure that symbolizes Buddha's enlightenment, often used as a reliquary.

*Churu (byu ru)*: coral.

*Dagtab (brtags tab)*: texts describing the appreciation of precious objects and stones.

*Datowoke (da 'bstod 'o bskod)*: a type of sandstone whetstone used to polish and shape stones.

*Dawang (da dbang)* or *Drepang ('dras pang)*: name of large shrine-shaped amulet box or *ga'u* worn by men in central and southern Tibet.

*Dolkhar mutik (dol khar mu tig)*: type of pearl from Amdo (north-eastTibet).

*Dorje (rdo rje)*: diamond and also 'diamond sceptre', a ritual object symbolizing enlightenment.

*Dorje phalam (rdo rje pha lam)*: diamond.

*Dug (gdugs)*: the Umbrella, symbol of protective power from the 'Eight Auspicious Emblems' see *Tashi tagye*.

*Dzi (gzi)*: bleached agate bead.

*Gaba (Nga ba)*: people living in the north east of eastern Tibet.

*Gara (mgar pa)*: a blacksmith.

*Gyalrong (rGyal rong)*: a goldfield in eastern Tibet.

*Gyaluche (rgya lu chas)*: costumes formerly worn by junior officials at the New Year, supposedly the same as those used by princes at the time of the Tibetan monarchy.

*Gya mutik (rgya mu tig)*: Chinese pearl.

*Gyuya (kyu ya)*: a large ring threaded through the queue of a man in eastern Tibet.

*Kashag (bKa' shags)*: the Tibetan cabinet of four ministers.

*Khedi (khal di)*: oval woman's *ga'u* (Lhasa name).

*Kherima (mkhal ri ma)*: oval woman's *ga'u* (southern Tibetan name).

*Kolentsi (ko len tsi)*, *Koranza (ko rnya dza)*: an abrasive powder (probably corundum) used in conjunction with a copper blade to cut and polish stones.

*Konchog sum (dkon mchog gsum)*: the three symbolic jewels of the Buddhist religion: the Buddha, the teachings and the religious community.

*Lam ber (lam 'ber)*: pitch used to hold sheet metal during embossing and for setting stones into bezels.

*Lu (klu)*: a water spirit.

*Man she (man shel)*: rock crystal (clear quartz).

*Mechag (mes lchags)*: tinder pouch.

*Nam chu wang den (rnam bcu dbang ldan)*: a monograph called the 'Sign of the All Powerful Ten' (comprising ten Sanskrit syllables representing the cosmos according to the *Kalachakra Tantra*. Worn as an amulet.

*Nul zowa (dngul bzo ba)*: a silversmith.

*Nya chi (nya phyis)*: mother-of-pearl.

*Nyarong (Nyag rong)*: goldfield in eastern Tibet.

*Pachog (pa lchog)*: the two braided hair knots worn formerly only by Lhasa officials of the fourth rank and above.

*Palbu (dpal be'u)*: the 'Endless Knot' symbol of interconnection from the 'Eight Auspicious Emblems'; see *Tashi tagye*.

*Perak (be rag)*: turquoise-covered headdress worn in parts of western Tibet and Ladakh.

*Pokhar (spos dkhar)*: a tree resin used to make the pitch on which objects are embossed, see *lam ber*.

*Poshe (spos shel)*: amber.

*Rab ney (rab gnas)*: the ceremony of consecration of a religious image.

*Rechi shing lo (ri pyi shing lo)*: 'coiled spring leaf', a type of scroll or *pata* used in eastern Tibet.

*Rigna (rigs lnga)*: ritual crown depicting the five meditation Buddhas.

*Ringyen (ring rgyan)*: the ornaments of the ancient kings worn by officials in the New Year ceremonies and said to have belonged to the kings of Tibet (7th to 9th centuries).

*Sadag (sa bdag)*: the spirits of the earth or soil.

*Ser dang (gSer mdangs)*: the reddish colour given to newly made gold articles by means of painting on a chemical.

*Serpon (gser dpon)*: official in charge of goldfields in western Tibet.

*Ser zowa (gser bzo ba)*: a goldsmith.

*So chi (so sbyis)*: long earring worn by lay officials.

*Sutumba (su tum ba), Sur dewa (sur de dba)*: rectangular woman's *ga'u* popular in western and southern Tibet.

*Ta zowa (phra bzoba)*: jeweller.

*Tagam (sta gam)*: ring of saddle shape.

*Tagor (skra gor), Tagab (ta ghab)*: small oval amulet box worn by lay officials of Fourth Rank and above.

*Tashi tagye (bkra shis rtags brgyad)*: the 'Eight Auspicious Emblems' of Buddhism.

*Tathi (pkra ti), Takhor (pkra khor)*: silver and inset stone clip ornament worn in the queues of men in eastern Tibet.

*Ten (rten)*: an image, painting or stupa (*chorten*), literally 'a support for religion'.

*Thok cha (thog lcags)*: small, ancient, cast-metal objects found in the fields and open country, believed to be of supernatural origin by Tibetans and often worn as amulets.

*Tranyi ('bra gnyis)*: an iron block with holes of varying sizes used for drawing silver wire.

*Treng wa (phreng ba)*: rosary.

*Trutok (bru mdog)*: hat ornament worn by officials of Fourth Rank up.

*Tsang (gTsang)*: southern Tibet.

*Tsha tser (tsha gser)*: fire or mercury gilding.

*Tsipatar (rtsis pa ta)*: the monster mask, a protective symbol derived from the Indian *kirttimukha* or 'Face of Glory.'

*Tubshi ('grub bzhis)*: square form of Lhasa women's amulet box or *ga'u* .

*U (dBus)*: central Tibet.

*Yangti (gyang ti)*: jade.

*Yid zhin norbu (yid bzhin nor bu)*: the 'Wish-Fulfilling Jewel' that grants all wishes.

*Yu (gyu)*: turquoise

*Yushe (gyu shad)*: the custom of a mother-in-law placing a turquoise on a new daughter-in-law's head after marriage.

*Zong (gzong)*: generic name for embossing punches and chasing chisels.

*Zurgyad (gzur brgyad)*: eight-armed Lhasa women's amulet boxes that appeared in the 1940s.

# Bibliography

Aaronson, D.(ed.), *Pearls*, New York, 2001.

Aitchison, J.E.T, *The Trade Products of Leh*, Calcutta, 1874.

Aris, M., *Bhutan, The Early History of a Himalayan Kingdom,* Warminster, 1979.

Bajracharya, P., 'The Tayo Bizakami', *Arts of Asia*, vol.31, no.3, pp.69–77, 2001.

Beall, C., and Goldstein, M.C., *Nomads of Western Tibet*, London,1989.

Beer, R., *The Encyclopedia of Tibetan Symbols and Motifs*, London, 1999.

Beguin, G., 'A propos d'une tiara d'Officiant Bouddhique', *La Revue de Louvre*, vol.34, no.3, pp.176–183, June 1984.

Bell, C.A., *The People of Tibet*, London, 1928, repr.1991.

Bellezza, J.V., ' *Thogchags*, Talismans of Tibet', *Arts of Asia,* pp.44–64, vol.28, no.3, May/June 1998.

Boyer, M., *Mongol Jewellery*, Copenhagen, 1952.

Camman, S., *Trade Through the Himalayas*, Princeton, 1951.

Cammann, S. van R., *China's Dragon Robes*, New York, 1952.

Clarke, J., 'A Regional Survey and Stylistic Analysis of Tibetan Non-Sculptural Metalworking, *c.*1850-–1959' (unpublished Ph.D. thesis) awarded by The School of Oriental and African Studies, London University, 1995.
—'Regional Styles of Metalworking', *Tibetan Art; Towards a Definition of Style*, (eds) J.C. Singer & P. Denwood, London, 1997, pp.278–289.
—'Gosains, Indian Trading Pilgrims

in Tibet', pp.278–289 in McKay, 1998.
—'The Tibetanisation of European Steel Stoves in Ladakh', *Ladakh: Culture, History and Development between Himalaya and Karakoram*, Aarhus, 1999, pls.28-9.
—'*Ga'u* – The Tibetan Amulet Box', *Arts of Asia*, vol.31, no.3, pp.45–67, Hong Kong, 2001.
—'Metalworking in dBus and gTsang, 1930–1977', *Tibet Journal*, vol. XXVII, no.1 & 2, pp.113–152, 2002.

Conze, E., *Buddhist Scriptures*, Harmondsworth, 1959.

Czuma, S.J., *Kushan Sculptures, Images from Early India*, Cleveland, 1978.

Dagyab, L.S., *Buddhist Symbols in Tibetan Culture: an investigation of the nine best-known groups of symbols*, Boston, 1995.
—*Tibetan Religious Art*, Wiesbaden, 1977.

Das, S.C.(ed.), *Journey to Lhasa and Central Tibet,* London, 1904.
—*A Tibetan-English Dictionary*, Alipore, 1902, repr. 1964.

Del Mare, C., *Le Vie del Corallo, Il corallo nella gioielleria etnica della Mongolia*, Torre del Greco, 1996.

Dilmar, Geshe, (De'u dmar dGe bshes), *Rig pa bzo yi gnas kyi las tshongs phren tsegs 'od rgur bsgyur ba spra phab 'od kyi snang brnyan,* 14th vol. of *Gangs can rig mdzod* series, Lhasa, 1990.

Ebbinghouse, D., and Winsten, M., 'Tibetan *dzi.(gZi)* Beads', *Tibet Journal*, vol. 13, pp.38–56, 1988.

Ekvall, R.B., and Cassinelli, C.W., *A Tibetan Principality. The Political System of SasKya*, New York, 1969.

Finot, L., *Les Lapidaires Indiens*, Paris, 1896.

Fogg, S., *Tibetan Manuscripts* catalogue 25, Sam Fogg Books and Manuscripts, London, 2001.

Gabriel, H., *Jewellery of Nepal*, Hong Kong, 1999.

Gajurel, C.L. and Vaidya, K.K., *Traditional Arts and Crafts of Nepal*, New Delhi, 1984.

Gerard, A., *An Account of Koonawur in the Himalayas*, London, 1841.

Gill, W., *The River of Golden Sand*, London, 1883.

Goepper, R., and Poncar, J., *Ladakh's Hidden Buddhist Sanctuary*, London, 1996.

Goldstein, M.C., *Nomads of Western Tibet: the survival of a way of life*, London, 1990.

Goldstein, M.C.(ed.), *The New Tibetan-English Dictionary of Modern Tibetan*, Berkeley, 2001.

Govinda, L.G., *Tibet in Pictures, Expedition to Western Tibet*, Berkeley, 1979, vol.2.

Grenard, F., *Tibet*, London, 1904.

Guenther, H.V., *Jewel Ornament of Liberation*, London, 1989.

Haarh, E., *The Yarlung Dynasty*, Copenhagen,1969.

Harcourt, J.P., 'The Himalayan Districts of Koolo, Lahoul & Spiti', *East India Punjab Records*, NS, 10, Lahore, 1874.

Heller, A., 'Some Preliminary Remarks on the Excavations at Dulan', *Orientations,* vol.29, no. 9, pp.84–92, October 1998.
—*Tibetan Art*, Milan, 1999.
—'Terma of Dolpo: The Secret Library of Pijor', *Orientations*, vol.32,

no.10, pp.64–67, December 2001.

—'Archaeological Artefacts from the Tibetan empire in Central Asia', *Orientations*, vol.34, no.4, pp.55–64, April 2003.

Henss, M., 'Wall Paintings in Western Tibet', pp.196–226 in Pal, 1996.

Heron, A.M., 'The Gem-Stones of the Himalaya', *The Himalayan Journal*, vol.2, pp. 21–28, April 1930.

Hodgson, B.H., 'On the Commerce of Nepal 1857', *Essays on the Languages & Religion of Nepal and Tibet*, Amsterdam, 1874, repr. 1971.

Hornell, J., *The Sacred Chank of India*, Madras Fisheries Bureau Bulletin, no.7, 1914.

Huc, E.R., and Gabet, J., *Travels in Tartary, Thibet and China* (2 vols), London, 1928.

Hughes, R.W., *Ruby & Sapphire*, Boulder, 1997.

Huxley, A., *The Doors of Perception*, New York, 1954.

Jones, S., *Tibetan Nomads*, Copenhagen, 1996.

Kaplanian, P., *Les Ladakhi du Cachemire*, Paris, 1981.

Kawaguchi, E., *Three Years in Tibet*, Madras, Benares, London 1909.

Khenrap, K.L., 'Ruthog District before the Chinese Occupation 1900-1958', *Tibet Journal*, vol.25, no.4, pp.33–77, 2000.

Klimburg-Salter, D., *Tabo: a Lamp for the Kingdom : early Indo-Tibetan Buddhist Art in the Western Himalaya*, Milan, 1997.

Kotturan, G., *The Himalayan Gateway: history and culture of Sikkim*, New Delhi, 1983.

Landon, P., *Lhasa* (2 vols), London, 1905. *Nepal* (2 vols), London, 1928.

Laufer, B., *Notes on Turquoise in the East*,

Publication 169, Field Museum of Natural History, Chicago, 1913.

Liu, R.K., *Collectable Beads*, Verona, 1995.

Lo Bue, E., 'Statuary metals in Tibet and the Himalayas: history, tradition and modern use', pp.33–69 in Oddy and Zwalf, 1981.

—'The Newar Artists of the Nepal Valley, an Historical Account of their activities in neighbouring areas with particular reference to Tibet', Part 1, *Oriental Art*, vol.31, pp.262–277, Autumn 1985; Part 2, vol.31, no.4, pp.408–420, Winter 1985/6.

Macdonald, A.(ed.), *Etudes tibetaines dediees a la memoire de Marcelle Lalou*, Paris, 1971.

—'Une lecture des pelliot Tibetain 1286, 1287, 1038, 1047, et 1290' pp.190–391 in *Etudes tibetaines*

Macdonald, A., and Stahl, A., *Newar Art*, Warminster, 1979.

Macdonald, D., *Twenty Years in Tibet*, London, 1929.

Mamgain, M.D., *Himachal Pradesh District Gazetteers*, vol.4, Lahul and Spiti, Chandigarh, 1975.

Markham, C.R., *Narratives of the Mission of George Bogle to Tibet and of the Journey of Thomas Manning to Lhasa*, London, 1879.

McKay, A.(ed.), *Pilgrimage in Tibet*, Richmond, 1998.

Migot, A., *Tibetan Marches*, London, 1955.

Mi pham rgya mtsho, J., *Bzo gnas nyer mkho'i za ma tog*, Xining, 1993.

Mukerjee, M., *Metalcraftsmen of India*, Calcutta, 1978.

Muller, C.C., and Raunig, W., *Der Weg Zum Dach der Welt*, Frankfurt, 1983.

Mullin, C., and Wangyal, P., *The Tibetans, two perspectives on Tibetan Chinese relations*, Minority Rights Group Report no.49, 1983.

Myers, D.K., and Bean, S.S.(eds), *From*

*the Land of the Thunder Dragon, Textile Arts of Bhutan*, London, 1994.

Nebesky Wojkowitz, R., 'Prehistoric beads from Tibet', *Man*, Journal of the Royal Anthropological Institute, no.52, pp.13–12, 1952.

Nieuhof, J., *An Embassy from the East India Company of the United Provinces to the Grand Tartar Cham Emperor of China*, London, 1673.

Normantas, P., *The Invincible Amdo Tibetans*, Helsinki, 1994.

Oddy, W.A., and Zwalf, W., *Aspects of Tibetan Metallurgy*, British Museum Occasional Paper, London, 1981.

Olson, E., *Catalogue of the Tibetan Collection and Other Lamaist Articles in the Newark Museum*, vol. 2, Newark, 1950.

—*Catalogue of the Tibetan Collection and Other Lamaist Articles in the Newark Museum*, vol. 5, Newark, 1971.

Pal, P., *Indian Sculpture*, vol. 2, Los Angeles, 1988.

Pal, P.(ed.), *On the Path to Void*, Mumbai, 1996.

Pal, P., and Fournier, L., *A Buddhist Paradise, The Murals of Alchi Western Himalayas*, Hong Kong, 1982.

Panfionovitch, Meyer and Dorje, G., *Tibetan Medical Paintings*, New York, 1992.

Parmee, E.A., *Kham and Amdo of Tibet*, New Haven, 1972.

Pogue, J.E., 'Turquoise', *Memoirs of the National Academy of Sciences*, vol.12, part 3, Washington, 1915.

Raha, M. K., and Mahato, S.N., *The Kinnawese of the Himalayas*, Calcutta, 1895.

Ramsay, H., *Western Tibet A Practical Dictionary*, Lahore, 1886.

Reynolds, V., *Tibet, a Lost World : the*

*Newark Museum Collection of Tibetan Art and Ethnography*, New York, 1978.
—*From the Sacred Realm, Treasures of Tibetan Art from the Newark Museum*, New York, 1999.

Rice, P., *Amber: the Golden Gem of the Ages*, New York, 1980.

Richardson, H., *Ceremonies of the Lhasa Year*, London, 1993.
—*High Peaks, Pure Earth*, London, 1998.

Richtsfeld, B., 'Der Amulettbehalter (*Ga'u*) und sein Inhalt', pp.288–307, in Muller & Raunig, 1983.

Rigzin, T., *Tibetan-English Dictionary of Buddhist Terminology*, Dharamsala, 1993.

Rizvi, J., *Ladakh: Crossroads of High Asia*, Delhi, 1998.

Rockhill, W.W., *Land of the Lamas*, Washington, 1891.
—*Diary of a Journey Through Mongolia and Tibet in 1891 and 1892*, Washington, 1894.
—*Notes on the Ethnology of Tibet*, Washington, 1895.

Roerich, N., *Trails to Inmost Asia*, New Haven, 1931.

Ronge, V., *Das Tibetische Handwerkertum von 1959*, Wiesbaden, 1978.

Sakya, J., and Emery, J., *Princess in the Land of Snows: the Life of Jamyang Sakya in Tibet*, Boston, 1990.

Salter, K., *The Silk Route and the Diamond Path*, Los Angeles, 1982.

Schafer, E.H., *The Golden Peaches of Samarkand: a study of T'ang exotics*, London, 1963.

Schroeder, V., *Indo-Tibetan Bronzes*, London, 1981.

Schweizer, H.R., *Der Schmied und sein Handwerk im Traditionellen Tibet*, Zurich, 1976.

Shakya, T., 'The Tibetanisation of Ladakh', *Tibetan Review*, pp.16–19, November 1982,

Shanghai Museum, *Treasures from Snow Mountains*, Shanghai, 2000.

Sharma, L.C., *Himachal Pradesh Rural Craft Survey*, Simla, 1967.

Singer, J.C., *Gold Jewellery from Tibet and Nepal*, London, 1996.
—*Sacred Visions*, New York, 1999.

Snodgrass, A., *The Symbolism of the Stupa*, New York, 1985.

Steinmann, B., 'The Opening of the *sBas Yul 'Bras ma'I gshongs* according to the Chronicle of the Rulers of Sikkim', pp.117–142 in McKay, 1998.

Stein, R.A., 'Du Recit au Rituel dans les Manuscrits de Touen-Houang', pp.479–556 in Macdonald(ed.), 1971.

Stephens, A., *Nepalese Jewellery* (unpublished), Travelling grant from Worshipful Company of Goldsmiths, London, 1985.

Stronge, S., *The Jewels of India*, Mumbai, 1995.

Tavernier, J.B., *Travels in India*, New Delhi, 1977 (reprint).

Teague, K., *From Tradition to Tourism in the Metalcrafts of Nepal*, (unpublished) Ph.D thesis, University of Hull, 1995.

Trotter, H., 'Account of the Pudit's Journey in Great Tibet from Leh in Ladakh to Lhasa, and of his return to India via Assam', *Journal of the Royal Geographical Society*, vol.47, 1877.

Tucci, G., *Tibet Ignoto*, Rome, 1978.

Tucci, G., and Ghersi, E., *Secrets of Tibet*, London, 1935.

Uhlig, H., *On the Path to Enlightenment*, Rietberg Museum, Zurich, 1995.

Untracht, O., *Traditional Jewellery of India*, London, 1997.

Van Spengen, W., *Tibetan Border Worlds*, London & New York, 2000.

Vitali, R., *The Kingdoms of Guge Puhrang*, Dharamsala, 1996.

Waddell, A., *Lhasa and its Mysteries*, London, 1906.

Wakefield, E., *Past Imperative: my Life in India*, London, 1966.

Walker-Watson, M.N., 'Turquoise: the Gemstone of Tibet', *Tibetan Review*, vol.18, no.67, pp.16–18, 1983.

Warikoo, K., *Central Asia and Kashmir: a Study in the Context of Anglo-Russian Rivalry*, New Delhi, 1989.

Weihreter, H., *Schmuck aus dem Himalaja*, Graz, 1988.

Whitfield, R., *The Art of Central Asia: The Stein Collection in the British Museum*, 3 vols., Tokyo, 1982–1985.

Wilson, M., 'The Colour of Stones', *Oriental Ceramic Society*, vol.62, 1997/8.

Windisch-Graetz, S. and G., *Juwelen des Himalaya*, Lucerne, 1981.

Woodford-Schmidt, C., 'The Sacred and the Secular: Jewellery in Buddhist Sculpture in the Northern Kushan Realm', pp.15–36 in Stronge, 1995.

Yeshi, Pugh(ed.), 'The Vajra and Bell and Beads', *Cho Yang: The Voice of Tibetan Religion and Culture*, vol.1, no.2, Dharamsala, 1987.

Yeshi, Pugh and Phipps, 'Precious Jewels of Tibet', *Cho Yang: The Voice of Tibetan Religion and Culture*, no.5, 1992.

Yogev, G., *Diamonds & Coral, Anglo-Dutch Jews and Eighteenth-Century Trade*, Leicester, 1978,

Yule, H.(ed.), *Cathay and the Way Thither*, 2 vols, 2nd Series, no.33, London, 1913.
—*The Book of Ser Marco Polo*, London, 1926.

Yule, H., and Burnell, A.C., *Hobson-Jobson: The Anglo-Indian Dictionary*, Ware, 1996 (reprint).

Yuthok, D.Y., *House of the Turquoise Roof*, New York, 1995.

# Acknowledgements

I would like to thank Tsepak Rigdzin (formerly of the Library of Tibetan Works and Archives, Dharamsala) for translating key Tibetan texts and Gene Smith and Burkhard Quessel for their helpful suggestions concerning these. Hannelore Gabriel has patiently answered many queries related to Nepalese jewellery and has been of great assistance with all matters Nepalese. I would also like to thank Monisha Ahmed for her time and effort in answering questions on jewellery wearing in Ladakh today and Mrs Karma Hardy for bearing with great equanimity an uncomfortable three-hour photo session dressed in heavy western Tibetan jewellery. Lastly, I owe a big vote of thanks to Erica Quan for diligent work in tracing references and to Joanna Whalley (Metals Conservation V&A) for her important analysis of stones and their cuts.

# Index